MW00889891

LEARN FRENCH FAST

FOR
ADULT BEGINNERS

Read, Write, Speak French In 30 Days

CONTENTS

DISCLAIMER NOTICE:

Please note that the information contained within this document is for educational and entertainment purposes only.

All effort has been executed to present accurate, up-to-date, reliable, complete information. No warranties of any kind are declared or implied. Readers acknowledge that the author is not engaged in the rendering of legal, financial, medical or professional advice. The content within this book has been derived from various sources.

Please consult a licensed professional before attempting any techniques outlined in this book.

By reading this document, the reader agrees that under no circumstances is the author responsible for any losses, direct or indirect, that are incurred as a result of the use of the information contained within this document, including, but not limited to, errors, omissions, or inaccuracies.

INTRODUCTION

Ah, French – the language of enchantment, the muse behind legendary literature, and the magic wand for artists to paint their visions on the canvas of expression. It's like stepping into a world where words dance and sentences sing. Complex? Indeed. Challenging? Absolutely. But fear not, for within this complexity lies a symphony of beauty waiting to be unraveled.

One could argue that it's only for its beauty, but the truth is that it's one of the most useful languages to learn. With over 300 million people speaking it, you're bound to bump into someone speaking French and knowing how to speak a local language is a great way to bond with the natives!

Picture yourself immersed in the allure of famous French football stars or captivated by the elegance of Paris showcased in a documentary. Imagine embarking on a journey to a French-speaking country, connecting with the locals through the power of their native tongue. The reasons to dive into this language are as endless as the romantic streets of Paris.

Perhaps you've heard the skeptics, dismissing French as too tough, its grammar a labyrinth. But hold on! Those doubters haven't experienced the magic tucked within these pages. You, my friend, have made a splendid choice!

As you embark on this journey, you'll find more than just chapters; you'll discover a comprehensive guide designed to elevate your understanding of French grammar, broaden your vocabulary, and immerse you in captivating short stories that breathe life into the language.

The initial section focuses on the fundamental aspects of French grammar, laying a solid foundation for your linguistic exploration. From the essential building blocks of pronouns, greetings, nouns, and articles to the nuances of descriptors and the exploration of crucial verbs like être and *avoir*, each chapter paves the way toward mastering the essentials. Navigate through French demonstratives, encounter more important verbs, and delve into practical topics such as eating, expressing likes and dislikes, negation, asking questions, and managing time, dates, and seasons.

Moving beyond grammar rules, the second section introduces practical words and phrases essential for everyday situations. Covering a spectrum from daily essentials and building connections to navigating shopping, dining out, and discussing travel, transportation, health needs, and emergencies, this section equips you with the tools needed for real-life communication.

In the third and final section, immerse yourself in the cultural richness of the French language through captivating short stories. From *"La Nouvelle Maison"* to *"L'Écharpe Rouge d'Emily,"* these narratives serve not only to reinforce your language skills but also to transport you into diverse scenarios, making the language a vibrant and integral part of your experience.

Whether you're a novice eager to grasp the fundamentals or an enthusiast looking to deepen your understanding, this book is crafted to guide you through the multifaceted world of French. So, are you ready to embark on this linguistic odyssey? **Alors, commençons!** (So, let's begin!)

We invite you to scan this "QR code"

By using the camera of your phone aiming at the QR code and clicking on the link that appears

to access your bonus content:

SCAN TO CLAIM YOUR BONUSES

OR

ENTER THIS URL IN YOUR WEB BROWSER:

bit.ly/speakfr1

(only use lowercase letters)

SECTION I:
GRAMMAR WORKBOOK

CHAPTER 1:

PRONOUNS AND GREETINGS

GOOD MORNING AND GOODBYE, FROM ME TO YOU

First things first! The first step to learning any language always begins with subject pronouns. In English, these are words like 'I', 'you', and 'they'. They indicate *who* exactly we're talking about and they're essential for everyday conversation! Without them, it would be impossible to describe ourselves, other people, and how events have affected us. They're some of the most basic building blocks of any language.

So let's take a look at what subject pronouns are in French!

1.1 Subject Pronouns

English	French	Pronunciation
I	je	[jə]
you (inf., sing.)	tu	[tu]
you (form., sing.)	vous	[voo]
he	il	[eel]
she	elle	[ehl]
we (m.) we (f.)	nous	[noo]
you (form. and inf., pl.)	vous	[voo]
they (m.)	ils	[eel]
they (f.)	elles	[ehl]

You'll notice that, in French, there are a lot more subject pronouns than in English! Aside from *who* they reference, they're also split up based on:

➲ formality of the situation;

➲ genders of the people you're talking about;

➲ quantity of subjects, i.e. whether you're just talking about one person or more.

Unlike in English, there are different French pronouns for singular 'you' and 'they'. Let's get a closer look, shall we?

Speak Abroad
Academy

Formal vs. Informal Pronouns

The use of the right singular 'you' depends on the formality of a situation. Try to remember that 'vous' is more formal, while 'tu' would be more casual. For example, if you were speaking directly to one person ('you'), you'd use the word **tu** in an informal situation and **vous** in a formal situation. But what exactly constitutes an informal or formal situation?

You'd use the formal word **vous** in interactions with people like:

- your boss
- a stranger or new acquaintance (unless you want to be casual straight away)
- a salesperson
- the cashier at the bank

You'd use the informal pronoun **tu** with:

- your friends
- your family
- children and animals
- other young people (if you want to create a closeness with them)

What if you're not sure whether to use *tu* or *vous*?

Situations may arise where you're not sure whether to go with the informal or formal pronoun. In this case, be safe and go with the formal **vous** at first. It's much better to be overly polite than to risk coming across as rude or overly casual. In doubt, the best way is to simply ask the other person if they prefer to be called with « tu » or « vous ».

> The masculine plural form **ils** refers to a group of males or to a group that includes both males and females. The feminine plural form **elles** only refers to a group of females. In other words, the default word for 'they' is **ils**, unless you're referring to a group of people that's entirely female.

> **Interesting fact:** In French, there is no neutral subject pronoun **because there is no neutral gender. Everything, from people and objects to abstract constructs, is either masculine or feminine.** You use **il** and **elle** for everything. I know, it would be like calling a shoe or a potato 'he' and 'she'. Quirky, right?

Now that we've built a preliminary foundation with the use of formal and informal pronouns, it's time for a little practice to really solidify that knowledge! Are you ready?

***Note on Abbreviations: masculine (m.); feminine (f.); informal (inf.); formal (form.); singular (sing.); plural (pl.)

Practice 1.1 Pronouns

A. Translate the following pronouns.

1. We (f.):
2. I:
3. They (f.):
4. They (m.):

5. You (inf.):
6. You (form.):
7. We:
8. They (co-ed.):

B. Write the correct subject pronoun.

1. _____ vais chez toi. (I'm going to your house.)
2. _____ sommes tes amis. (We — (m.) — are your friends.)
3. _____ êtes les meilleurs. (You — (m. inf. pl.) — are the best.)
4. _____ sont amis. (They — (m.) — are friends.)
5. _____ es une femme. (You — (sing. inf.) — are a woman.)

C. Replace the names/pronouns between brackets with an adequate pronoun.

1. {They (m.)} _____ vont manger (will eat) au restaurant (at the restaurant).
2. {You – form.} _____ êtes invité au mariage (are invited to the wedding).
3. _____ {Elise and you/inf.}, voulez-vous aller au mariage (want to go to the wedding)?
4. {Thomas and I} _____ avons une surprise (have a surprise).
5. {Samuel} _____ vit au Québec (lives in Quebec).

D. What would you say with each of the following, **tu** or **vous**?

1. Your grandmother
2. A coworker
3. A flight attendant
4. Your boss
5. A little boy

6. Your professor
7. A repair person
8. Your cousin
9. Your best friend
10. Your father-in-law

E. Say which pronoun you would use according to the situation: **tu** or **vous**

1. You tell your close friend: «_____ sais très bien cuisiner. » (*You're very good at cooking*)
2. You ask the waiter at a restaurant when your table will be ready. He answers: « _____ êtes les suivants. » (*You're next*).
3. You ask your siblings if they want to come with you to the park: « _____ voulez venir avec moi ? » (*Do you want to come?*)
4. You tell your friends that they're your best friends: « _____ êtes mes meilleurs amis » (*You are my best friends*)
5. You compliment your doctor: « _____ êtes si intelligent. » (*You're so intelligent*).

1.2 Greetings and Polite Expressions

As we mentioned earlier, your word choices will vary depending on the formality of the situation. This applies not only to pronouns but also to longer exchanges, like greetings. In English, formality and informality matter too! For example, you probably wouldn't enter a formal meeting with your boss and say, "Hey, what's up?"

In French, it's no different. You'll have different greetings for different types of situations. The words might essentially mean the same thing, but the choices convey whether you're familiar or unfamiliar with the person or people you're addressing.

Informal Greeting

Consider the following informal greeting between Amélie and François, two young housemates who go to the same college. Since they're both peers, they'll use informal language with each other, even if they're not that close.

Amélie: Salut, François.
(*Hi, François.*)

François: Salut Amélie. Ça va ?
(*Hi, Amélie. How's it going?*)

Amélie: Bien. Et toi ?
(*Good. And you?*)

François: Ça va bien ! À tout à l'heure.
(*Very good! See you later.*)

Amélie: Ciao.
(*Bye.*)

Formal Greeting

Now, let's look at a formal greeting between Monsieur Delort and Madame Morgane. Monsieur Delort is a security guard at Madame Morgane's apartment building. Even though they're both middle-aged, they would use formal language with each other, since they don't know each other well, and they aren't exactly peers.

Monsieur Delort: Bonjour, Madame Morgane.
(*Good afternoon, Madame Morgane.*)

Madame Morgane: Bonjour, Monsieur Delort. Comment allez-vous ?
(*Good afternoon, Monsieur Delort. How are you?*)

Monsieur Delort: Très bien, merci. Et vous ?
(*Very good, thank you. And you?*)

Madame Morgane: Très bien, merci. Au revoir.
(*Very good, thanks. Goodbye.*)

Monsieur Delort: Au revoir.
(*Goodbye.*)

Both the informal and formal greetings essentially say the same thing, but they'll use different words in the formal exchange to express politeness. That said, some words and phrases will remain the same. You can still say **bien** or **très bien** to say *you're doing well* or *very well*, and in either situation, you can still say **au revoir** to say *goodbye*.

Vocabulary: Basic Greetings

English	French	Pronunciation
Hi	**Salut**	[sah-lu]
How's it going?	**Ça va ?**	[sah vah]
Good	**Bien**	[byahn]
And you?	**Et toi ?**	[ay twah]
Very good	**Très bien**	[tray byahn]
See you later	**À la prochaine**	[ah lah pro-shen]
Goodbye	**Au revoir**	[oh rə-vwahr]
Bye	**Ciao**	[chaw]

Tip: Ça va ? and **Et toi ?** are greeting expressions used in informal situations, with people you know well, on a first-name basis.

Vocabulary: Other Greetings

English	French	Pronunciation
Good morning/Hello	**Bonjour**	[bohn-zhoor]
Good afternoon	**Bonjour**	[bohn-zhoor]
Good evening, good night	**Bonsoir**	[bohn-swahr]
Good night	**Bonne nuit**	[buhn nwee]
Mr.	**Monsieur (M.)**	[muh-syuh]
Mrs.	**Madame (Mme)**	[mah-dahm]
Miss	**Mademoiselle (Mlle)**	[mah-də-mwah-zayl]
How are you?	**Comment allez-vous?**	[koh-mahn tah-lay voo]

English	French	Pronunciation
And you?	**Et vous ?**	*[ay voo]*
See you soon	**À bientôt**	*[ah byah-toh]*
See you tomorrow	**À demain**	*[ah də-mahn]*
Have a good afternoon	**Bon après-midi**	*[bohn ah-prey mee-dee]*

Did you notice that « Bonjour » is used at different times of the day? It's because this is the most common way to say 'Hello' in French. However, « Bonsoir » means 'Good evening' (greetings) and 'Good night' (when you leave the room). But if you wanted to wish someone good night (when you leave) or when you're going to bed, it's « Bonne nuit » = 'Sweet dreams').

> **Tip: Comment allez-vous ?** and **Et vous ?** are used to address someone with whom you have a more formal relationship, like your boss or a salesperson – or to address a group of people, of course. (with plural « vous »)

1.3 Language Etiquette

Next, we have the 'magic' words and phrases that will help you address others politely in everyday life. Remember to say 'please' and 'thank you' in French, just as you do in English.

English	French	Pronunciation
Thanks / Thank you	**Merci**	*[mayr-see]*
Thanks a lot / Thank you very much	**Merci beaucoup**	*[mayr-see boh-koo]*
You're welcome	**De rien**	*[də ryahn]*
Please	**S'il te plaît**	*[seel tə play]*
Please (form. or to address a group)	**S'il vous plaît**	*[seel voo play]*
It's nothing / No problem	**Pas de problème**	*[pah də proh-blaym]*
Excuse me / Pardon me (to get someone's attention or to apologize to someone for something you did)	**Pardon / Désolé**	*[par-dohn]/ [day-zaw-lay]*
Excuse me (to get someone's attention or to apologize to someone for something you did)	**Excusez-moi**	*[ayx-ku-zay mwah]*

Practice 1.3 Language Etiquette

A. Choose the most appropriate response from the list on the right to the following greetings or expressions:

1. Merci beaucoup. _____   a) Bonsoir.
2. Bonjour. _____   b) De rien.
3. Ça va ? _____   c) Bonjour, comment allez-vous ?
4. A la prochaine. _____   d) Bien, et toi ?
5. Bonsoir. _____   e) Au revoir.

B. What might these people say to each other if they met or passed each other at the time given? Choose between Salut / Bonjour / Bonsoir. Multiple options may apply.

1. Laura and Matthew at 2.00 p.m.
2. Mary and her boss at 7.00 a.m.
3. You and your friend at noon.
4. Joe and Ann at 7.00 p.m.
5. You and your Math teacher at 11 a.m.

C. Match the situation with what you say if it happens

1. You accidentally bump into a person on the street.   a) Excusez-moi.
2. You thank someone for helping you with your luggage.   b) Pas de problème.
3. You're trying to get the attention of a waiter.   c) Merci beaucoup.
4. Your friend is grateful that you're lending him some money.   d) S'il vous plaît.
5. An elderly woman thanks you for helping her cross the street.   e) De rien.

D. Choose the most appropriate response to the following statements or questions

1. Merci beaucoup.   a) Au revoir.
2. Ça va ?   b) Pas de problème.
3. Comment allez-vous ?   c) Bien, et toi ?
4. Ciao.   d) Très bien, merci.
5. Désolé.   e) De rien.

E. Complete the following dialogue with the right greeting or phrase.

1. YOU: Salut François, _____ [1] ?
2. François: Bien, merci, _____ [2] ?
3. YOU: Très _____ [3].
4. François: Ciao. _____ [4] demain.
5. YOU: _____ [5].

CHAPTER 2:

NOUNS AND ARTICLES

THE DOG AND THE CAT

2.1 The Gender of Nouns and the Singular Definite Article

Now that we've dipped our toes into pronouns, let's navigate the captivating world of nouns in French. Nouns are the building blocks of language representing objects, places, and things.

Unlike English, all nouns in French are either masculine or feminine. This doesn't mean that objects are perceived as having literal gender differences, of course, but rather, they are just classified into different groups.

Some of these are straightforward, such as le garçon and la fille, which mean 'the boy' and 'the girl' respectively. As you'd expect, **garçon** is a masculine noun and **fille** is a feminine noun. Although they're different words, **le** and **la** both mean 'the' – they simply apply to different genders. You would never ever say « **la garçon** » or « **le fille** » as it would be grammatically incorrect.

It's easy with people, but less so with objects and places. To speak fluent French, you'll need to get used to the genders of different nouns. For example, you'll need to remember that *a book* is masculine while *a photograph* is feminine.

To make this easier, picture this: learning French is like having a conversation with objects, and they come in two fashionable outfits (masculine and feminine). Imagine strolling through a linguistic wardrobe where a book confidently sports a bow tie (m.), while a photograph gracefully dons a flowing gown (f.). So, when you're chatting *en français*, it's not just about words; it's a sartorial adventure through the gendered closets of nouns!

Therefore, it's important that the definite article (*the*) should always agree with the gender of the noun. This is a hard one for English speakers, because we only have one definite article — 'the' — and don't have to worry about the rest! With practice, you'll get the hang of it.

Singular Masculine Nouns

As we mentioned earlier, the masculine singular noun uses the definite article « **le** ». This shows we are referring to just one thing, place, or object. Don't worry about plural nouns for now; we'll get to those later.

Watch out, though. If the noun that follows starts with a vowel or a silent 'H', you need to use « **l'** » instead. So, don't say « le homme », but « l'homme ».

English	French	Pronunciation
The man	l'homme	[lohm]
The friend (male)	l'ami	[lah-mee]
The boy	le garçon	[luh gahr-sohn]
The son	le fils	[luh fees]
The brother	le frère	[luh frayr]
The grandfather	le grand-père	[luh grahn-pehr]
The uncle	l'oncle	[lohn-kluh]
The cat	le chat	[luh shah]
The dog	le chien	[luh shyahn]
The book	le livre	[luh leevr]
The telephone	le téléphone	[luh teh-leh-foh-nə]
The building	le bâtiment	[luh bah-tee-mahn]
The youngster	le jeune	[luh zhuhn]

Singular Feminine Nouns

The feminine singular noun uses the definite article « **la** ».

English	French	Pronunciation
The person	la personne	[lah pehr-sohn]
The woman	la femme	[lah fahm]
The mother	la mère	[lah mayr]
The friend (female)	l'amie	[lah-mee]
The girl	la fille	[lah feey]
The sister	la sœur	[lah sur]
The grandmother	la grand-mère	[lah grahn-mehr]
The aunt	la tante	[lah tahnt]
The cat (female)	la chatte	[lah shaht]
The dog (female)	la chienne	[lah shyayn]
The house	la maison	[lah may-zon]
The food	la nourriture	[lah noo-ree-tur]
The car	la voiture	[lah vwah-teur]
The chair	la chaise	[lah shayz]

Nouns and articles

Having established a preliminary understanding of the usage of noun genders, let's reinforce this knowledge through some hands-on practice! Are you prepared?

Practice 2.1 Gender of Nouns

Instructions: What's the appropriate masculine or feminine form of the definite article (the) for each noun? And while you're at it, try translating the word by yourself, these ones are almost identical to their English counterparts

1. photo (f.)
2. hôpital (m.)
3. télévision (f.)
4. programme (m.)
5. système (m.)

6. problème (m.)
7. planète (f.)
8. hôtel (m.)
9. personne (f.)
10. animal (m.)

2.2 Plural Nouns and the Plural Definite Article

Plural Nouns

So far, we've only covered singular nouns. That is, just one object, place, or thing. But what if you wanted to refer to multiple friends, not just one friend? Or many books, not just a single book? This is where plural nouns come in.

In English, we usually indicate that there is *more* than one thing by adding –s to the end of the word, like 'friends' or 'books'. In French, plurality is also indicated by modifying the ending of the word.

In French, plural nouns end in either an **–s** or **–x**.

If the French singular noun ends in EAU, AU, or EU, you'll add an **–x** to the end of the word. For example, with the nouns...

tableau (picture) → **tableaux**

cheveu (hair) → **cheveux**

However, there are always a few exceptions:

un pneu (a tire) → **des pneus**

un landau (a pram) → **des landaus**

bleu (blue) → **bleus**

Don't worry. We'll be explaining the proper use of 'des' in a short while

If the ending is AL, it will add **–aux.** For example...

cheval (horse) → **chevaux**

But again, there are a few exceptions

un bal (a ball)   →   **des bals**

un festival (a festival)   →   **des festivals**

When it's not **–x**, the plural noun will end in **–s**. For example, when you want to indicate more than one friend, you would then use the word **amis**, and for more than one table, you would use **tables**.

ami   →   ami<u>s</u>

table   →   table<u>s</u>

Fingers crossed, you're catching the rhythm of this dance by now! If you're referring to multiple pencils, you'd use the word **crayons**. And for multiple mouths, you would use the word **bouches**.

You might be noticing that something is missing – the definite article. How do we say 'the tables' or 'cities'?

Just like the nouns, the definite articles are also modified to indicate plurality.

The masculine definite article **le** becomes **les**.

The feminine definite article **la** becomes **les**.

For example...

<u>le</u> chien   →   <u>les</u> chiens

<u>la</u> maison   →   <u>les</u> maisons

Remember that in French, if we're referring to multiple people that consist of both females and males, we use the masculine plurality by default. So, you would use the term **les amis** when referring to your friends if your friends include female and male people.

To clarify...

les amis = male friends OR male friends + female friends

Keep in mind that, just like in English, we don't always need to use the definite article. In English, the definite article is the word 'the,' and in French, this is **le, la** (or **l'**) and **les**. So, when do you need to use the definite article?

First, let's just quickly go over what the point of the definite article is. Let's use an English example.

If you have a salad in your fridge that you really need to eat before it goes bad, you would say: 'I need to eat *the* salad.' Using the definite article indicates that you have a specific salad in mind. It's already there and it's just waiting to be eaten!

However, if you feel like you've been eating too much fast food lately, you might say: "I need to eat *a* salad." In this case, you don't have a specific salad in mind, you just need to eat any salad. That's why we call it the *definite* article, because there is more sureness and specificity implied.

These rules about when to use the definite article also apply to French – but a couple of extra ones are added on top. Let's summarize!

In French, the definite article (**le**, **la**, **les**) is used...

- like English, to refer to a specific person or thing. **La femme** d'Adam est Eve (*Eve is Adam's woman*).

- unlike English, to refer to something in a conceptual or broad sense. **J'aime la viande** (*I like meat*) or **J'aime la musique** (*I like music*).

- unlike English, to refer to parts of your own body. **Je me suis cassé le bras** (*I broke my arm*).

Now that we've built a preliminary foundation in the use of plural nouns, it's time for a little practice to really solidify that knowledge! Are you ready?

Practice 2.2 Plural Nouns

A.   Write the plural version of each singular noun. When you finish, read each pair out loud.

1.   L'homme _____
2.   L'amie _____
3.   La conversation _____
4.   L'animal _____
5.   Le système _____

6.   Le chat _____
7.   La maison (the house) _____
8.   Le train (the train) _____
9.   La ville (the city) _____
10. Le médecin (the doctor) ___

B.   Write the singular version of each plural noun. When you finish, read each pair out loud.

1.   Les chiens _____
2.   Les télévisions _____
3.   Les femmes _____
4.   Les chiennes _____
5.   Les hôpitaux _____

6.   Les filles _____
7.   Les garçons _____
8.   Les salades _____
9.   Les bâtiments _____
10. Les voitures _____

2.3 The Indefinite Article

Now that we've chatted about the definite article, it's time to meet its more mysterious cousin — the indefinite article. Curious to find out more? Let's dive into the world of indefinite articles together! Remember when we talked about the difference between 'I need to eat *the* salad' and 'I need to eat *a* salad'? As you can probably guess, it's in '*a* salad' where the indefinite article is used. We use the indefinite article to refer to a thing that is non-specific.

In English, the indefinite article is *a* or *an*. In French, the indefinite articles are…

Masculine, singular: **un** (*a/an*)   Feminine, singular: **une** (*a/an*)

Masculine, plural: **des** (*some*)   Feminine, plural: **des** (*some*)

For example:

Une amie (*a female friend*) →   **des amies** (*some female friends*)

Un garçon (a boy)   →   des garçons (some boys)

To summarize, you only use the indefinite article (**un**, **une**, **des**) when:

⊃   You want to identify someone or something as part of a class or a group:
    c'est un animal (*it's an animal*)

⊃   You want to refer to something in a non-specific way:
    Un bateau est fait pour naviguer (*A boat is for sailing*) or
    C'est une jeune femme (*She's a young woman*).

Quick Recap

	MASCULINE SINGULAR NOUNS	MASCULINE PLURAL NOUNS	FEMININE SINGULAR NOUNS	FEMININE PLURAL NOUNS
DEFINITE ARTICLES	**Le** chien (the male dog)	**Les** chiens (the male dogs or the female and male dogs)	**La** chienne (the female dog)	**Les** chiennes (the female dogs)
INDEFINITE ARTICLES	**Un** chien (a male dog)	**Des** chiens (some male dogs or some female and male dogs)	**Une** chienne (a female dog)	**Des** chiennes (some female dogs)

Un and **une** (both *a* and *an*) can mean *one* as well as *a* or *an*. You will understand which one it means based on the context. For example, **un** garçon (*a boy*) vs. J'achète **un** manteau (*I buy one coat*).

Nouns and articles

Now that we've laid the groundwork for handling plural nouns and indefinite articles, it's time to roll up our sleeves and put that knowledge into action! Ready for a bit of practice to make those concepts stick?

Let's dive in and elevate that French fluency!

Practice 2.3 Indefinite Articles

A. Turn these singular nouns with indefinite articles into plural nouns with their indefinite articles.

1. un grand-père : _____
2. un livre : _____
3. un chien : _____
4. une femme : _____
5. un étudiant : _____

6. un médecin : _____
7. un hôtel : _____
8. un train : _____
9. un chat : _____
10. une ville : _____

B. Translate the following:

1. The (male and female) students: _____
2. The planets: _____
3. A doctor: _____
4. Some photographs: _____
5. The woman : _____
6. The sisters : _____
7. Some (male and female) friends: _____
8. A dog : _____
9. The mother : _____
10. Some houses: _____

C. Complete the sentences with **le**, **la**, **les**, or **un**, **une**, **des**.

1. _____ maison de Samuel.
2. J'ai trouvé (*I found*) _____ pièces de monnaie (*coins*).
3. C'est _____ tête (*head*) de François.
4. C'est _____ trace de pied (*footprint*).
5. Ce sont _____ amies de ma soeur. (*They are some friends of my sisters.*)
6. J'aime _____ poulet. (*I like chicken.*)
7. Je ramène _____ gâteau chez toi. (*I'm taking a cake to your house.*)
8. Samuel va acheter _____ boissons pour la fête. (*Samuel is buying the drinks for the party.*)
9. Comment était _____ pièce de théâtre ? (*How was the play?*)
10. Elle a acheté _____ nouvelle chemise. (*She bought a new shirt.*)

D. Do you remember what these nouns are in English? Remember to translate them with the definite or indefinite article that precedes them.

1. La femme _____
2. La maison _____
3. Le poulet _____
4. Le garçon _____
5. Les frères _____
6. Le médecin _____
7. Le train _____
8. Les planètes _____
9. Un chat _____
10. Des chiens _____
11. Le téléphone _____
12. Les boissons _____
13. Un programme _____
14. Des systèmes _____
15. Les livres _____

E. Circle the right answer. You need to decide whether the article should be singular or plural:

1. [La / Les] mère de Thomas est sympathique. *(Thomas's mother is nice.)*
2. Je veux [un / des] livres pour apprendre. *(I want some books to learn.)*
3. Je veux [les / une] nouvelle télévision. *(I want a new TV.)*
4. [Le / Des] chat est dans la maison. *(The cat is in the house.)*
5. Il a brisé[les / une] fenêtre. *(He broke a window.)*
6. J'aime [les / la] fleurs. *(I like flowers.)*
7. J'ai parlé avec [le / des] directeur de l'école. *(I spoke with the head of the school.)*
8. Amélie a vu [les / un] chien. *(Amelie saw a dog.)*
9. Je mets [les / une] clés dans le sac. *(I put the keys in the bag.)*
10. As-tu [les / le] clés de la maison ? *(Do you need your house keys?)*

F. Complete with the right definite or indefinite article (**le / la / les / un / une / des**).

1. Washington est _____ ville aux États-Unis. *(Washington is a city in the USA.)*
2. La rue Voltaire est _____ rue de ton village. *(Voltaire St is a street from your village.)*
3. Paris est _____ capitale de la France. *(Paris is the capital of France.)*
4. _____ maison de Clara est grande. *(Clara's house is big.)*
5. _____ pape vit à Rome. *(The pope lives in Rome.)*

CHAPTER 3:

DESCRIBING PEOPLE, PLACES, AND THINGS
THE BLACK CAT

3.1 Singular Adjectives

Remember what a noun is? It's a person, place, or thing, like 'house' or 'table'.

Sometimes it isn't enough to simply mention the object or subject – sometimes, it's necessary to describe the object or subject. This is where adjectives come in. We use adjectives to describe the nouns we're talking about. For example, we could say that a person is beautiful and smart – or that a table is big or small.

In French, we usually put the adjective *after* the noun that we're describing, except when we're talking about:

- **Beauty**: When something or someone is beautiful, pretty, or handsome, e.g. **beau** ('beautiful or handsome').
- **Age**: When something or someone is young, new, or old, e.g. **jeune** ('young').
- **Goodness**: When something is good or bad, e.g. **bon** ('good').
- **Size** – When something or someone is small, big, long, or fat, e.g. **petit** ('small').

For example, to say 'the friendly cat', this would look like **le gentil chat**. As you can guess, the word **gentil** means friendly and it is the adjective.

You can remember this with the acronym BAGS.

However, in most other cases, the adjective goes after the noun.

Adjectives are also used to describe other qualities, like the nationality of something or someone. For example, to say 'French food', we would say **nourriture française.**

Furthermore, the ending of an adjective will also change depending on:

- the gender of the noun;
- the singularity or plurality of the noun.

So, if you have a feminine singular noun like **la photo** (*the photo*), you would need to use a feminine singular adjective like **jolie** (*beautiful*) to describe it. In this case, you would say **la jolie photo** to mean 'the beautiful photo'.

Masculine Singular Forms of Adjectives

Here are some examples of adjectives for singular masculine nouns. Remember, some of these will go *before* the noun!

English	French	Pronunciation
The tall student	le grand étudiant	[luh grahn ay-tew-dee-ahn]
The short boy	le petit garçon	[luh puh-tee gahr-sohn]
The good brother	le bon frère	[luh bohn frehr]
The bad dog	le mauvais chien	[luh moh-vay shyan]
The fat cat	le gros chat	[luh groh shah]
The interesting book	le livre intéressant	[luh leevr an-tay-ray-sahn]
The friendly boy	le gentil garçon	[luh zhahn-tee gahr-sohn]
The unfriendly teenager	l'adolescent antipathique	[lah-doh-leh-sahn ahn-tee-pa-teek]
The small book	le petit livre	[luh puh-tee leevr]
The hardworking father	le père fort	[luh pehr fohr]
The beautiful sofa	le joli sofa	[luh joh-lee soh-fa]
The old man	le vieil homme	[luh vee-ay ohm]

Feminine Singular Forms of Adjectives

But what if you're not referring to a masculine noun? Sometimes, you need to describe a female student as tall, not just a male student! Notice how the endings of the adjectives change in the following list.

English	French	Pronunciation
The tall (female) student	la grande étudiante	[lah grahnd ay-tew-dee-ant]
The short girl	la petite fille	[lah puh-teet fee]
The kind sister	la gentille sœur	[lah zhawn-teey suhr]
The bad (female) dog	la mauvaise chienne	[lah moh-vayz shyayn]
The fat (female) cat	la grosse chatte	[lah grohs shat]
The interesting story	l'histoire intéressante	[lees-twahr an-tay-reh-sahnt]
The friendly girl	la gentille fille	[lah zhawn-teey fee]
The unfriendly (female) youngster	l'adolescente antipathique	[lah-doh-leh-sahnt ahn-tee-pah-teek]
The small house	la petite maison	[lah puh-teet meh-zohn]

English	French	Pronunciation
The strong mother	**la mère forte**	*[lah mehr fohrt]*
The beautiful city	**la jolie ville**	*[lah joh-lee vil]*
The old woman	**la vieille femme**	*[lah vee-ay fahm]*

Endings that Don't Change

In many cases, you need to add « e » at the end of a masculine adjective to create the feminine version, unless there's already an « e » at the end.

Le grand garçon becomes **la grande fille.**

Le jeune homme becomes **la jeune femme.**

However, sometimes, you're lucky because you don't need to change the ending of an adjective. This makes it a little easier! For the following adjectives, the ending remains the same for masculine and feminine nouns.

English	French	Pronunciation
The weak boy	**le faible garçon**	*[luh febl gar-sawn]*
The poor man	**le pauvre homme**	*[luh po-vr ohm]*
The loyal friend	**l'ami fidèle**	*[lah-mee fee-dayl]*
The difficult conversation	**la conversation difficile**	*[la kawn-ver-sa-syon dee-fee-seel]*
The friendly professor	**l'aimable professeur**	*[lay-ma-bluh pro-feh-sur]*
The young girl	**la jeune fille**	*[la zhuhn fee-yuh]*

Ready to rock the world of singular masculine and feminine adjectives?

Let's jump into practice, making these concepts your language allies and boosting your French fluency!

Practice 3.1 Singular Adjectives

A. Translate the English adjective into its French equivalent. Make sure it matches the noun.

1. La _____ fille *(tall)*
2. Le _____ homme *(poor)*
3. Le chien _____ *(loyal)*
4. La _____ femme *(beautiful)*
5. Le problème _____ *(difficult)*

6. Le _____ garçon *(good)*
7. Le _____ grand-père *(old)*
8. Le livre _____ *(interesting)*
9. La _____ amitié *(strong)*
10. La tête _____ *(small)*

B. Translate the English adjective into its French equivalent. Make sure it matches the noun.

1. La _____ fille *(poor)*
2. La _____ nourriture *(good)*
3. La _____ ville *(small)*
4. Le _____ garçon *(friendly)*
5. Le _____ chien *(old)*

6. Le _____ étudiant (bad)
7. L'amie _____ (intelligent)
8. La chienne _____ (loyal)
9. Le garçon _____ strong
10. La _____ femme (fat)

C. Write the opposite adjectives to the one in the sentences below.

1. Le programme facile _____
2. Le petit garçon _____
3. Le mauvais restaurant _____
4. La fille antipathique _____
5. L'homme fort _____

3.2 Plural Form of Adjectives

Bet you saw this one coming, right? When the noun is plural and refers to multiple things, the adjectives must be modified to agree with the plurality.

When an adjective refers to more than one masculine noun, we add **–s** to the end of the adjective. For example...

Grand → **grands** *(tall)*

Pauvre → **pauvres** *(poor)*

If the noun you're describing is feminine, then instead you'll add **–es** to the end of the adjective. For example...

Grande → **grandes** (tall)

Watch out for some exceptions! For instance, some words ending with **–x** do not change.

Un homme heureux → **des hommes heureux**

Incidentally, the feminine would be **– euse(s)** in that case

Une femme heureuse → **des femmes heureuses**

Remember this rule: if the French singular adjective ends in EAU, AU, or EU, you'll add an **–x** to the end of the word. This works for adjectives too!

Un beauc garçon → **des beaux garçons**

But here, the feminine is **-elle** instead. It's an exception:

Une belle femme → **des belles femmes**

Don't worry, at this stage, you only need to focus on the general rule.

Speak Abroad
Academy

Let's practice this!

Practice 3.2 Plural Adjectives

A. Write the plural form of each of the following nouns and adjectives.
1. La grande tomate (tomato) _____
2. Le petit homme _____
3. Le chien intelligent _____
4. La fille forte _____
5. La personne gentille _____
6. La petite ville _____
7. Le chat mince *(thin)* _____
8. La femme heureuse _____
9. Le livre difficile _____
10. L'excellente *(excellent)* nourriture _____

B. Complete the sentence with the correct form of the adjectives:
1. Les _____ livres (intéressant)
2. La grand-mère _____ (travailleur)
3. La _____ ville (beau)
4. Les _____ livres (petit)
5. Les _____ sofas (joli)
6. Les _____ sœurs (bon)
7. Les _____ chats (gros)
8. Les enfants _____ (gentil)

3.3 Adjectives of Nationality

As mentioned earlier, nationalities are also adjectives. They describe that a person or thing originates from a specific country.

Like the other adjectives we've discussed, they are also modified depending on the gender of the noun and plurality.

For example, we would say...

The man is Tunisian. → L'homme est tunisien.

The men are Tunisian. → Les hommes sont tunisiens.

And for feminine nouns, we would say...

The woman is French. → La femme est française.

The women are French. → Les femmes sont françaises.

Notice how these rules work just like they do for the other adjectives! So, how do we refer to other nationalities in French?

English	French	Pronunciation
French	**français(e)**	[frahn-say] / [frahn-sess]
English	**anglais(e)**	[ahn-glay] / [ahn-gless]
American	**américain(e)**	[ah-may-ree-kahn] / [ah-may-ree-kahn]
Spanish	**espagnol(e)**	[eh-spahn-yol]
German	**allemand(e)**	[ahl-mahn] / [ahl-mahn-d]
Italian	**italien(ne)**	[ee-tahl-yen]
Portuguese	**portugais(e)**	[por-tu-gay] / [por-tu-gess]
Japanese	**japonais(e)**	[jah-poh-nay]
Chinese	**chinois(e)**	[shee-nwah]
Tunisian	**tunisien(ne)**	[tyoo-nee-zyen]

> **Tip:** In French, you must capitalize the names of nationalities when they are used as nouns, but not when they are used as adjectives.

Having established an understanding of the usage of adjectives of nationality, let's reinforce this knowledge through some hands-on practice! Are you ready?

Practice 3.3 Nationality

Write the nationality next to each noun, making it match in gender and number.

1. La statue de la liberté est
2. La Tour Eiffel est
3. Big Ben est
4. La Tour de Pise est
5. Le musée du Prado est

3.4 Describing a Person

In French, there's more than one way to write a descriptive sentence – just like in English. You can say 'the intelligent woman' or you can say 'the woman is intelligent.'

So far, we've only discussed how to say sentences like 'the intelligent woman', i.e. **la femme intelligente.** Now, let's try a different way of using these descriptors.

To say a singular someone or something *is* something, you use the French word **est.** This means that 'the woman is intelligent' would become « **la femme** <u>est</u> **intelligente** ».

Of course, you don't always have to specify 'the woman', you can also use pronouns to indicate who you're talking about. In this case, just replace the noun with the pronoun. To simply say 'she is intelligent', you translate this to « **elle est intelligente** ».

Thankfully, the words 'is' and **est** are only different by two letters, so this should be somewhat easy to remember! You'll also be glad to hear that you use the word **est** no matter if you're talking about a feminine or masculine noun. For example, 'he is intelligent' would be « **il est intelligent** ».

Now, let's jazz up our descriptive skills by diving into hands-on practice with adjectives when describing someone!

Are you up for the fun challenge?

Practice 3.4 Describing People

A.   Which adjectives are the most appropriate for each sentence?
1.   La fille est [vieille / jeune]
2.   Le bébé *(baby)* est [petit / grand]
3.   Le livre est [intéressant / fort]
4.   Le garçon est [drôle *(funny)* / excellent]
5.   Le chien est [loyal / pauvre]

B.   Choose which adjective is most appropriate depending on the gender agreement.
1.   La femme est [intelligente / intelligent]
2.   Le chat est [gros / grosse]
3.   La fleur est [belle / beau]
4.   La mère est [gentil / gentille]
5.   L'oncle est [vieux / vieille]

C.   Translate the following into French:
1.   Marc is French: _____
2.   The boy is tall: _____
3.   The girl is intelligent: _____
4.   The man is kind: _____
5.   The woman is pretty: _____

D.   Do you remember where these famous people are from?
1.   Napoléon Bonaparte est _____
2.   Kim Kardashian est _____
3.   Daniel Craig est _____
4.   Marco Polo est _____
5.   Coco Chanel est _____

CHAPTER 4:

MORE DESCRIPTORS
THE YELLOW BRICK ROAD

4.1 More Adjectives

It's time to pause the rulebook and dive into a symphony of new words! Let's unleash the power of French adjectives, and watch as your vocabulary transforms into a kaleidoscope, painting the world, people, and experiences with vibrant hues of expression. By learning more French adjectives, you'll be able to describe the world, the people around you, and the experiences you have in greater detail. So, are you ready to splash some linguistic colors? Let the wordplay begin!

We will begin with some useful everyday adjectives that you'll need to know.

Essential Everyday Adjectives

English	French	Pronunciation
Fast	**rapide**	*[rah-peed]*
Slow	**lent(e)**	*[lahnt]*
Expensive	**cher (chère)**	*[shayr]*
Easy	**facile**	*[fa-seel]*
Famous	**célèbre**	*[seh-leh-br]*
Long	**long (longue)**	*[lohn] / [lohn-g]*
Short	**court(e)**	*[koor] / [koor-t]*
Young	**jeune**	*[zhuhn]*
Elderly	**vieux (vieille)**	*[vyo] / [vyeh]*
Pretty	**beau (belle)**	*[boh] / [bel]*
Ugly	**laid/moche (laide)**	*[leh] / [mohsh] / [led]*
Happy	**joyeux (joyeuse)**	*[zhwah-yuh] / [zhwah-yuhz]*
Sad	**triste**	*[treest]*
Rich	**riche**	*[reesh]*
New	**nouveau (nouvelle)**	*[noo-voh] / [noo-vell]*
Blond	**blond(e)**	*[blon] / [blond]*
Dark-haired	**brun(e)**	*[bruhn] / [brun]*
Delicious	**délicieux (délicieuse)**	*[day-lee-syuh] / [day-lee-syooz]*

You might be wondering what these adjectives would look like in a sentence. Let's use them with some nouns we used in prior chapters.

Le problème facile	(*the easy problem*)
La moto rapide	(*the fast motorcycle*)
Le problème facile	(*the easy problem*)
La fille célèbre	(*the famous girl*)
La joyeuse femme	(*the happy woman*)
L'homme triste	(*the sad man*)
Le garçon brun	(*the dark-haired boy*)
La délicieuse nourriture	(*the delicious food*)
La courte leçon	(*the short lesson*)
Le long train	(*the long train*)

In a nutshell, these adjectives add color and detail to familiar nouns. Now, it's your turn to play with these combinations and paint your own linguistic canvas. Ready to give it a go? Take out your notepad because practice makes perfect!

Diving into the Colors

Colors in French, just like other adjectives, play a crucial role. Apply the rules you've mastered for adjectives to colors as well — treat them the same way, positioning them after the noun. Let's keep the color palette of your French language vivid and vibrant!

Explore the table below to acquaint yourself with fundamental colors in French. If you're an art enthusiast accustomed to the world of colors, you might recognize a few. French is renowned in the realm of artist's paints and makeup products, making it a familiar language for color aficionados.

Basic Colors

English	French	Pronunciation
White	**blanc**	*[blahn]*
Black	**noir**	*[nwar]*
Red	**rouge**	*[roozh]*
Blue	**bleu**	*[bluh]*
Yellow	**jaune**	*[zhawn]*
Green	**vert**	*[vehr]*
Gray	**gris**	*[gree]*
Pink	**rose**	*[rohz]*
Brown	**marron**	*[mah-ron]*
Orange	**orange**	*[oh-rahzh]*

We've seen that adjectives that already end with an **–e** do not change with their gender. It's the same for colors. Here, let's take a look!

English	French (m.)	French (f.)
White	**blanc**	**blanche**
Black	**noir**	**noire**
Red	**rouge**	**rouge**
Blue	**bleu**	**bleue**
Yellow	**jaune**	**jaune**
Green	**vert**	**verte**
Gray	**gris**	**grise**
Pink	**rose**	**rose**
Brown	**marron**	**marron**
Orange	**orange**	**orange**

Nope, this is no mistake. Marron doesn't change with its gender. And it doesn't change with plural either. Quite impressive!

une maison marron – des maisons marron

Additionally, here are more examples of how to use colors with a noun:

La planète rouge   (*the red planet*)
Le crayon noir   (*the black pencil*)
Le chat blanc   (*the white cat*)
Le sofa jaune   (*the yellow sofa*)
La chaise verte   (*the green chair*)
La moto bleue   (*the blue motorcycle*)
La maison rose   (*the pink house*)
La chienne marron   (*the brown dog*)

To modify these colors for plurality or multiple nouns, add **–s** (if it's masculine) or **–es** (if it's feminine) to the end of each adjective. For example...

Les planètes rouges   (*the red planets*)
Les crayons noirs   (*the black pencils*)
Les chats blancs   (*the white cats*)
Les sofas jaunes   (*the yellow sofa*)
Les chaises vertes   (*the green chairs*)
Les motos bleues   (*the blue motorcycles*)
Les maisons roses   (*the pink houses*)
Les chiennes marron   (*the brown dogs*)

Practice 4.1 Adjectives

A. Find the right adjective for the following nouns according to whether the noun is masculine or feminine.

1. La voiture est _____ (nouvelle / nouveau)
2. La femme est _____ (joyeuse / joyeux)
3. Le chien est _____ (gros / grosse)
4. Le garçon est _____ (méchant /méchante) *(naughty)*
5. Le livre est _____ (vieux / vieille)
6. La maison est _____ (chère / cher)
7. Le bébé est _____ (grand / grande)
8. La fille est _____ (lent / lente)
9. Le chat est _____ (bruyant / bruyante) *(noisy)*
10. Le train est _____ (long / longue)

B. Complete the following phrases translating the color adjective in English to French.

1. La fleur _____ *(yellow)*
2. La maison _____ *(blue)*
3. La chaise _____ *(orange)*
4. La main _____ *(white)*
5. La chatte _____ *(black)*
6. Le crayon _____ *(gris)*
7. Le sofa _____ *(green)*
8. Le téléphone _____ *(pink)*
9. Le chien _____ *(brown)*
10. La tomate _____ *(red)*

C. Complete the sentences in French below by claiming the opposite of what the first part of the sentence says. **English example: The cat is slow and the dog is fast.**

1. L'homme est lent et la femme est _____
2. Le chat est noir et la chienne est _____
3. La voiture est grande et l'enfant est _____
4. L'enfant est gros et la fille est _____
5. Le père est vieux et la mère est _____

D. All these people and things are complete opposites. Complete the sentences in French.

1. Rachel est petite et jeune. Thomas est _____.
2. Emily est belle et riche. Sarah est _____.
3. La maison est nouvelle et grande. La voiture est _____.
4. Jennifer est triste et lente. Stuart est _____.
5. L'examen est difficile. Le jeu vidéo -video game est _____.

4.2 Demonstrative Adjectives

We've talked mainly about common adjectives so far. Now, let's talk about demonstrative adjectives. You've probably noticed that we're throwing around some very official linguistic terminology here. Let me just say that although it's important for you to be introduced to official terms like 'demonstrative adjective', you don't have to remember them *as long as you remember the rule itself.*

So, let's talk about demonstrative adjectives.

These are words like 'this' or 'that', which draw attention to specific nouns (singular or plural). You know what purpose they serve in English, and it's essentially the same in French.

When we use these words, they go *before* the noun, just like in English, and they also change if we're talking about multiple nouns. This is like the difference between 'this' and 'these'. For example, you would say **ce chien** for 'this dog' and **ces chiens** for 'these dogs'.

And of course, they also need to be modified if you're talking about a feminine noun, like for example, **cette maison** (this house) and **ces maisons** (these houses).

this	**ce (m.)** **cet (+ vowel) (m.)**	*[sə] [sayt]*	**cette (f.)**	*[sayt]*
these	**ces (m.)**	*[say]*	**ces (f. pl.)**	*[say]*

Now let's see if you're with me so far.

Practice 4.2 Demonstrative Adjectives

A. Beatriz and her friend go shopping. Check out what they say about the clothes, using the demonstrative adjectives in their correct form. Use **est** (*is*) or **sont** (*are*) depending on whether the subject is singular or plural.

Example: robe (dress) / rouge (red) → **cette robe est rouge.**

1. **(m.)** manteau *(coat)* / beau → _____

2. **(f.)** chaussures *(shoes)* / chères→ _____

3. **(f.)** chemise *(shirt)* / douce *(soft)* → _____

4. **(f.)** bottes *(boots)* / élégantes *(elegant)* → _____

5. **(m.)** chapeau *(hat)* / propre *(clean)* → _____

*Très is an adverb that means **very**. Adverbs go before adjectives and verbs. Check out some more adverbs here:

très (very)	+ adjective/adverb	Ces fleurs sont **très** belles. *(Those flowers are very beautiful.)*
beaucoup (a lot)	+ verb	Samuel voyage **beaucoup**. *(Samuel travels a lot.)*
assez (quite)	+ adjective/adverb/verb	Elle marche **assez** rapidement *(She walks quite fast.)*
peu (not a lot)	+ adjective/adverb/verb	Martin mange **peu**. *(Martin doesn't eat a lot.)*
trop (too much)	+ adjective/adverb/verb	Amélie parle **trop**. *(Amélie talks too much.)*

B. Complete these sentences with **ce, (cet), cette**, or **ces**.
1. _____ (*This*) planète est très grande.
2. _____ (*This*) train est grand.
3. _____ (*This*) moto est nouvelle.
4. _____ (*These*) jeunes sont sympathiques.
5. _____ (*This*) étudiant est jeune.

4.3 Describing People and Adjectives in the Plural Form

Remember when we talked about using **est** to describe a singular noun? Like, for example, **la femme est intelligente** to say 'the woman is intelligent'?

It also becomes necessary to describe plural nouns in the same way. In English, 'is' becomes 'are' when we're talking about plural nouns, like in the sentence 'the books are boring'. We've done some of this in French already, but let's get more acquainted with these rules.

In French, **est** becomes **sont**.

Instead of...

Il est : *he (m.) is*

Elle est : *she (f.) is*

You would say...

Ils sont : *they (m.) are*

Elles sont : *they (f.) are*

Just like **est**, you use the word **sont** regardless of whether the noun is feminine or masculine.

For example:

They (a group of men) are thin. → **Ils sont** minces.

They (a group of women) are intelligent. → **Elles sont** intelligentes.

Now, you know how to say 'he/she/it is' and 'they are'! Try and practice this with different adjectives.

Vocabulary: The Neighborhood

Time to expand your vocabulary! Let's look at some nouns that you'll encounter in your typical neighborhood, town, and city.

English	French	Pronunciation
Tree	arbre (m.)	[ahr-br]
Flower	fleur (f.)	[flur]
Street	rue (f.)	[ree]
Post office	Poste (f.)	[post]
Bakery	boulangerie (f.)	[boo-lahn-zhuh-ree]
Supermarket	supermarché (m.)	[soo-per-mar-shay]
Office	bureau (m.)	[byoo-roh]
Movie theatre	cinéma (m.)	[see-nay-mah]
Park	parc (m.)	[pahrk]
Garden/yard	jardin (m.)	[zhar-dan]
School	école (f.)	[ay-kohl]
College/university	université (f.)	[ew-nee-ver-see-tay]
Train station	gare (f.)	[gahr]
Subway station	station de métro (f.)	[sta-syon də meh-tro]
Church	église (f.)	[ay-gleez]
Airport	aéroport (m.)	[ay-roh-port]
Museum	musée (m.)	[myoo-zay]
Bar	bar (m.)	[bahr]
Restaurant	restaurant (m.)	[res-tow-rah]
Building	bâtiment (m.)	[bah-tee-mahn]
Shop	boutique (f.)	[boo-teek]

Now that we understand how to use adjectives in the plural form to describe people, it's time to put ourselves to the test!

Practice 4.3 Describing Nouns

A. Imagine you're showing your friend around your block from your car. Point out some places of interest, completing the sentences with the right form of *this*: **ce, cette, ces, cet**.

1. _____ maison est très grande.

2. _____ bâtiment (*building*) est la Poste (*post office*) et _____ arbre est très vieux

3. _____ rue (*street*) est nouvelle et _____ chiens sont dangereux (*dangerous*).

4. _____ église (*church*) est vieille.

B. Rewrite these sentences using the right form of the demonstrative adjective **est** or **sont** (depending on whether the subject is singular or plural).

1. Ces bâtiments _____ très vieux.
    (These buildings are very old.)

2. L'aéroport _____ nouveau, mais les gares _____ vieilles.
    (The airport is new but the train stations are old.)

3. Le musée _____ près du supermarché.
    (The museum is next to the supermarket.)

4. Les arbres _____ grands et le jardin _____ petit.
    (The trees are big and the garden is small.)

5. La boulangerie _____ mon endroit préféré.
    (The bakery is my favorite place.)

6. Les boutiques ici _____ américaines. Les boutiques là bas _____ françaises. *(The shops here are American. The shops there are French.)*

7. Les parcs _____ beaux.
    (The parks are beautiful.)

8. L'école _____ proche de l'université.
    (The school is next to the university.)

9. Les fleurs _____ roses.
    (The flowers are pink.)

10. Les livres _____ chers parce que la bibliothèque _____ vieille.
    (The books are expensive because the library is old.)

Common Mistake: When using the word **personne**, avoid using a masculine adjective, even if the sex of the person you are referring to is male. **Personne** always agrees with a **feminine adjective**:

X WRONG	✓ CORRECT
Alain est une bo**n** personne.	Alain est une bon**ne personne**.
Martin est une personne travailleu**r**.	Martin est une **personne** travailleu**se**.
Samuel est une genti**l** personne.	Samuel est une genti**lle personne**.

CHAPTER 5:

THE VERB ÊTRE

TO BE OR NOT TO BE

5.1 Present Tense of Être

I hope you remember the words **est** and **sont**. They mean 'is' and 'are', which are essentially the same thing, but one is singular and the other is plural. The French words **est** and **sont** are all rooted in the same verb être, which means 'to be'.

In English, we use the words 'is' and 'are' for basically everything. You use it to say both 'the car is red' (description) and 'the car is here' (location), even though you're describing pretty different types of qualities. It's a very useful verb, and it's just as useful in French.

However, there is one big difference!

In French, there are more than two variations of this important word.

You already know **est** and **sont** ('is' and 'are'), which can be used to say **il/elle est** (he/she/it is) and **ils/elles sont** (they are). But what if you wanted to say 'we are' or 'I am'? To refer to different pronouns, you'll need to make modifications.

Let's take a look at these modifications!

Être *(to be)*			
je	**suis**	nous	**sommes**
tu	**es**	vous	**êtes**
il		ils	
elle	**est**	elles	**sont**

Here are some examples of how we use these words in sentences.

I am intelligent.	→	**Je suis** intelligent.
I am a cat.	→	**Je suis** un chat.
I am young.	→	**Je suis** jeune.

We are intelligent.	→	**Nous sommes** intelligents.
We are cats.	→	**Nous sommes** des chats.
We are happy.	→	**Nous sommes** heureux.

You are intelligent (inf.).	→	**Tu es** intelligent.
You are a cat (inf.).	→	**Tu es** un chat.
You are old (inf.).	→	**Tu es** vieux.

You are intelligent (form.).	→	**Vous êtes** intelligent.
You are a cat (form.).	→	**Vous êtes** un chat.
You are beautiful (form.).	→	**Vous êtes** beau.

You all are intelligent (pl.).	→	**Vous êtes** intelligents.
You all are cats (pl.).	→	**Vous êtes** des chats.
You all are funny (pl.).	→	**Vous êtes** drôles.

They are intelligent (m., co-ed.).	→	**Ils sont** intelligents.
They are cats (m., co-ed.).	→	**Ils sont** des chats.
They are poor (m., co-ed.).	→	**Ils sont** pauvres.

They are intelligent (f.).	→	**Elles sont** intelligentes.
They are cats (f.).	→	**Elles sont** des chattes.
They are kind (f.).	→	**Elles sont** gentilles.

Profession

We also use these verbs to indicate someone's profession. However, you'll notice that, in French, this works differently from English.

In English, you would say, 'I am a doctor' or 'You are a teacher'.

In French, you would say, '*Je suis médecin*' or '*Tu es professeur*'.

When indicating someone's profession in French, omit the definite and indefinite article. You simply *are* the profession.

The table below introduces some French words for other professions so you can get used to practicing subject pronouns with the verb **être**.

Common Professions

English	French	Pronunciation
Doctor	**médecin**	*[med-sahn]*
Teacher	**professeur**	*[proh-fess-uhr]*
Painter	**peintre**	*[pahn-truh]*
Chef	**chef**	*[shehf]*

English	French	Pronunciation
Engineer	ingénieur/ ingénieure	[ahn-zhey-nyuhr]
Artist	artiste	[ahr-teest]
Baker	boulanger/ boulangère	[boo-lahn-zhay] / [boo-lahn-zhair]
Secretary	secrétaire	[seh-kruh-tair]
Waiter	serveur/ serveuse	[sehr-vuhr] / [sehr-vuhz]
Nurse	infirmier/ infirmière	[ahn-feer-myay] / [ahn-feer-myair]
Writer	écrivain(e)	[ay-kree-vahn] / [ay-kree-vehn]
Police officer	policier	[poh-lees-yay]
Lawyer	avocat(e)	[ah-voh-kah] / [ah-voh-kaht]
Manager	gérant(e)	[zhay-rahn] / [zhay-rahnt]
Fire fighter	pompier	[pohn-pyay]
Cashier	caissier/ caissière	[keh-syay] / [keh-syehr]
Pharmacist	pharmacien(ne)	[far-mah-syan] / [far-mah-syen]
Driver	chauffeur	[shoh-fuhr]

Ready to take the stage with your linguistic performance? Time to put yourself to the test!

Practice 5 Être

A.   Read the following dialogue in 'New in the City' and then answer the questions.

New in the City / (Nouveau dans la ville)

THOMAS: Excusez-moi, êtes-vous d'ici ? Je suis perdu.
ADELINE: Non, je suis une touriste.
THOMAS: Êtes-vous française ?
ADELINE: Oui, je suis française.
THOMAS: Oh ! Je suis français aussi. Mais mon ami Paul est anglais.
ADELINE: Je suis perdue aussi. New York, c'est grand !
THOMAS: Vous êtes perdue aussi ? Ah ! Voici une carte !

Glossary:

d'ici: from here
perdu: lost
touriste: tourist
aussi: too/also

mais: but
mon ami: my friend
voici: here
carte: map

1. Who is lost? (Qui est perdu ?) _____
2. Who is French? (Qui est français ?) _____
3. Who is English? (Qui est anglais ?) _____
4. Why are they lost? (Pourquoi sont-ils perdus ?) _____
5. What did they find to help them? (Qu'est-ce qu'ils ont trouvé pour les aider ?)

   _____

B. Where are these famous people from? Use the word **est** to say what nationality they are.

Anglais/e (English)   Français/e (French)   Espagnol/e (Spanish)
Italien/ne (Italian)   Portugais/e (Portuguese)   Mexicain/e (Mexican)
Américain/e (American)   Autrichien/ne (Austrian)   Allemand/e (German)

   Example: David Beckham est anglais.
   1. Luciano Pavarotti _____
   2. Frida Kahlo _____
   3. Johnny Depp _____
   4. Albert Einstein _____
   5. Coco Chanel _____
   6. Rafael Nadal _____
   7. Cristiano Ronaldo _____
   8. Paul McCartney _____
   9. Arnold Schwarzenegger _____
   10. Taylor Swift _____

C. Complete the following sentences with the appropriate form of the verb être. Pay attention to the subjects and subject pronouns that they follow.
   1. Nous _____ heureux d'être ici. (*We are happy to be here.*)
   2. Tu _____ mon meilleur ami. (*You are my best friend. – inf.*)
   3. Les filles _____ en train de jouer en haut. (*The girls are playing upstairs.*)
   4. Je _____ dentiste. Tu _____ médecin. (*I am a dentist. You are a doctor.*)
   5. Mon mari _____ très grand. (*My husband is very tall.*)
   6. Les enfants _____ en train de jouer dehors. (*The boys are playing outside.*)
   7. Ils _____ des nouveaux étudiants. (*They are new students.*)
   8. Nous _____ en train de manger au parc. (*We are eating at the park.*)
   9. Aujourd'hui, elle _____ au travail. (*Today, she is at work.*)
   10. Aujourd'hui, il _____ en train de jouer au football. (*Today, he is playing football.*)
   11. Excusez-moi, Madame, vous _____ très belle. (*Excuse me, Madame, you are very beautiful.*)
   12. Vous (pl.) _____ des invités magnifiques. (*You all are fantastic guests.*)
   13. Je _____ au supermarché. (*I am at the supermarket.*)
   14. Melissa _____ dans la voiture. (*Melissa is in the car.*)
   15. La vache _____ dans le jardin! Elle _____ en train de manger les fleurs! (*The cow is in the garden! She is eating the flowers!*)

16. Ils _____ les meilleurs danseurs au monde. (*They are the best dancers in the world.*)
17. Vous (pl.) _____ invités à ma soirée. (*You all are invited to my party.*)
18. Les femmes _____ très rapides. (*The women are very fast.*)
19. Tu _____ ma fille préférée. (*You are my favorite daughter.*)
20. Maman, je _____ ta fille unique! (*Mom, I'm your only daughter!*)

D. Add the correct subject pronouns and forms of the verb être next to the following characters.

Example: <u>She is</u> slow. <u>Elle est</u> *lente.*

1. <u>We are</u> happy. _____ contents.
2. <u>They (m.) are</u> very intelligent. _____ très intelligents.
3. <u>I am</u> tired. _____ fatigué.
4. <u>You (inf.) are</u> the best. _____ le meilleur.
5. <u>You (form.) are</u> at the bank. _____ à la banque.
6. <u>We are</u> old. _____ vieux.
7. <u>They (f.) are</u> young and beautiful. _____ jeunes et belles.
8. <u>They (co-ed.) are</u> at school today. _____ à l'école aujourd'hui.
9. <u>You (inf.) are</u> taller than me. _____ plus grand que moi.
10. <u>You (plur.) all are</u> very loud. _____ très bruyants.

E. Write the following English sentences in French.
1. Anna is at the museum. _____.
2. We are outside. _____.
3. Elsa and Jane are at school. _____.
4. They *(co-ed.)* are at the bank. _____.
5. He is at the supermarket. _____.
6. We are in the car. _____.
7. You *(inf.)* are happy. _____
8. I am young and beautiful. _____.
9. You *(f.)* are very intelligent. _____.
10. You *(pl.)* are at the supermarket. _____.

F. Fill the blanks with the missing French words, using everything we've learned in the book so far.
1. Nous _____ dehors dans _____. (We <u>are</u> outside in <u>the car.</u>)
2. Elle _____ dans le jardin. Il _____ dans _____ (She <u>is</u> in the garden. He <u>is</u> in <u>the house.</u>)
3. Je _____ serveur. Elle _____ secrétaire. (I <u>am</u> a waiter. She <u>is</u> a secretary.)
4. Peter _____ français. Et Emily? _____ aussi! (Peter <u>is</u> French. And Emily? <u>She is French</u> too!)
5. Tu _____ *(inf.)* belle et je _____ intelligent. (You <u>are</u> pretty and I <u>am</u> intelligent.)

Speak Abroad
Academy

CHAPTER 6:

THE VERB AVOIR

I HAVE NINETY-NINE PROBLEMS AND FRENCH ISN'T ONE

6.1 Present Tense of Avoir

In the previous chapter, you discovered the most important verb of all, meaning 'to be'. The next verb that's essential for you to learn is *avoir*, which means 'to have'. This useful verb indicates that you possess something, though this is not always physical. In fact, *avoir* is also used to say how old you are, what you need, and form other tenses.

But for now, let's focus on constructing simple sentences with *avoir*.

Avoir *(to have)*			
je	**ai**	nous	**avons**
tu	**as**	vous	**avez**
il		ils	
elle	**a**	elles	**ont**

Notice something interesting about the first-person singular conjugation of *avoir*? That's right, *je* becomes *j'* because the next letter begins with a vowel. This happens a lot in French. So instead of saying *je ai* (incorrect!), you say *j'ai* to say 'I have'.

Here are some examples of how to use *avoir* in sentences.

I have a dog.	→	J'ai un chien.
I have a big house.	→	J'ai une grande maison.
I have an expensive dress.	→	J'ai une robe chère.
We have a dog.	→	Nous avons un chien.
We have a big house.	→	Nous avons une grande maison.
We have an important meeting.	→	Nous avons une réunion importante.
You have a dog. (inf.)	→	Tu as un chien.
You have a big house. (inf.)	→	Tu as une grande maison.
You have a new television. (inf.)	→	Tu as une nouvelle télévision.

You have a dog (form.)	→	Vous avez un chien.
You have a big house. (form.)	→	Vous avez une grande maison.
You have a black umbrella. (form.)	→	Vous avez un parapluie noir.

You all have a dog. (pl.)	→	Vous avez un chien.
You all have a big house. (pl.)	→	Vous avez une grande maison.
You all have a lot to do today.(pl.)	→	Vous avez beaucoup de choses à faire aujourd'hui.

They have a dog.	→	Ils ont un chien.
They have a big house.	→	Ils ont une grande maison.
They have a beautiful car.	→	Ils ont une jolie voiture.

They have a dog. (f.)	→	Elles ont un chien.
They have a big house. (f.)	→	Elles ont une grande maison.
They have a delicious cake. (f.)	→	Elles ont un gâteau délicieux.

Everyday Objects

I think it's time to get ready to sprout new French words! Let's add a splash of excitement to your vocabulary palette and watch it blossom. Here are some everyday objects that you can practice using *avoir* with.

Essential Everyday Objects

English	French	Pronunciation
Computer	ordinateur (m.)	[or-dee-nah-teur]
Mobile phone	téléphone portable (m.)	[tay-lay-fohn por-tah-bluh]
Newspaper	journal (m.)	[zhoor-nahl]
Bag	sac (m.)	[sahk]
Scarf	écharpe (f.)	[ay-sharp]
Keys	clés (f.)	[klay]
Cup/Glass	verre (m.)	[vehr]
Bottle	bouteille (f.)	[boo-tay]
Money	argent (m.)	[ar-zhahn]
Note	billet (m.)	[bee-yay]
Passport	passeport (m.)	[pass-pohr]
Notebook	carnet (m.)	[kahr-nay]
Pen	stylo (m.)	[stee-loh]
Umbrella	parapluie (m.)	[pah-rah-plwee]
Sunglasses	lunettes de soleil (f.)	[loo-net duh soh-lay]

Speak Abroad
Academy

Family Members

Of course, we can't forget some of the most important people that we *have*. Our family members!

English	French	Pronunciation
Family	**famille (f.)**	*[fa-mee]*
Mother	**mère (f.)**	*[mehr]*
Father	**père (m.)**	*[pehr]*
Sister	**sœur (f.)**	*[suhr]*
Brother	**frère (m.)**	*[frehr]*
Grandmother	**grand-mère (f.)**	*[grahn-mehr]*
Grandfather	**grand-père (m.)**	*[grahn-pehr]*
Uncle	**oncle (m.)**	*[ohn-kluh]*
Aunt	**tante (f.)**	*[tahnt]*
Husband	**époux (m.)**	*[ay-poo]*
Wife	**épouse (f.)**	*[ay-pooz]*
Daughter	**fille (f.)**	*[fee]*
Son	**fils (m.)**	*[fees]*
Cousin	**cousin (m.)**	*[koo-zanh]*
Niece	**nièce (f.)**	*[nee-ess]*
Nephew	**neveu (m.)**	*[nuh-vuh]*

With avoir firmly grasped, let's dive into hands-on practice! Ready to flex those French language muscles? Let's get started!

Practice 6.1 Present Tense of Avoir

A. Write the appropriate form of **avoir** for the following sentences. This time let's bring the definite article (*le, la*) back into the mix!

1. _____ une idée intéressante. (*We have an interesting idea.*)
2. _____ une voiture blanche. (*I have a white car.*)
3. _____ la plus belle écharpe. (*You have the most beautiful scarf – inf.*)
4. _____ un billet de train. (*I have a train ticket.*)
5. _____ une jolie sœur. (*She has a pretty sister.*)
6. _____ trois ordinateurs. (*They have three computers – co-ed.*)
7. _____ un chien drôle. (*He has a funny dog.*)
8. _____ une mère gentille. (*They have a kind mother – f.*)
9. _____ une grande famille. (*You have a big family – form.*)
10. _____ une fille intelligente et un grand fils. (*We have an intelligent daughter and a tall son.*)

B. Based on the context of the sentence, identify whether to use être or **avoir** to fill in the blanks. Make sure to match the subject pronoun in the parentheses and conjugate the verb accordingly!

1. Aujourd'hui, _____ fatigué. *(I)*

2. _____ un rendez-vous important. *(You – form.)*

3. _____ une jolie épouse. _____ heureux. *(He)*

4. _____ une grande maison. _____ riche. *(She)*

5. _____ un gâteau délicieux. *(They – co-ed.)*

6. _____ médecins. *(We)*

7. _____ deux chiens. *(I)*

8. _____ jeune ! _____ un téléphone portable. *(You – inf.)*

9. _____ gentilles. Et _____ belles aussi! *(They – f.)*

10. _____ une vieille voiture. *(We)*

C. Fill in the blanks and finish the French translations of these English sentences, using the correct form of **avoir**.

1. *I'm running late! I have an appointment at noon.*
   Je suis en retard ! _____ un rendez-vous à midi.

2. *They have a big family. That's why they have a big house (co-ed.)*
   _____ une grande famille. C'est pour ça qu' _____ une grande maison.

3. *She has three cats and he has four dogs.*
   _____ trois chats et _____ quatre chiens.

4. *You have a kind brother (form.).*
   _____ un gentil frère.

5. *They have too many cars (f.).*
   _____ trop de voitures.

6. *We have a son who is a doctor.*
   _____ un fils qui est médecin.

7. *I have a pink flower. It's for my mother.*
   _____ une fleur rose. C'est pour ma mère.

8. *You have a newspaper? You're an old man (inf.)!*
   _____ un journal ? Tu es un vieil homme !

D. Paul and Francine are getting to know each other better. Read the following French dialogue and answer the questions.

PAUL : As-tu une grande famille ?

FRANCINE : Oui. J'ai trois sœurs et quatre frères. Et toi ?

PAUL : J'ai une petite famille. Je suis enfant unique.

FRANCINE : As-tu des cousins ?

PAUL : Oui, j'ai un cousin.

Francine : Wow, tu as une petite famille !

PAUL : Oui. Mais j'ai cinq chiens. Ils sont ma famille aussi.

Francine : Je comprends. Mes chats sont ma famille aussi.

Glossary

Trois : three

Quatre : four

Cinq : five

Enfant unique : only child

Ma famille : my family

Je comprends : I understand

Mes chats : my cats

1. How many sisters does Francine have?
   (*Combien de sœurs a Francine ?*)
2. How many siblings does Paul have?
   (*Combien de frères et sœurs a Paul ?*)
3. Who has one cousin?
   (*Qui a un seul cousin ?*)
4. Who has dogs? How many?
   (*Qui a des chiens ? Combien ?*)
5. Who has cats?
   (*Qui a des chats ?*)

6.2 Other Uses for Avoir

In French, you use 'I have' to indicate more than just your possessions. It's also used to say that you are hungry or thirsty. For example...

I have hunger. (I am hungry)	→	**J'ai** faim.
I have thirst. (I am thirsty)	→	**J'ai** soif.
We have hunger. (We are hungry)	→	Nous **avons** faim.

She has thirst. (She is thirsty)	→	Elle **a** soif.
He has hunger. (He is hungry)	→	Il **a** faim.
You have thirst. (You are thirsty)	→	Tu **as** soif.

You get the idea! In French, you don't say that you *are* thirsty or hungry. You say that you *have* thirst or hunger, which means you always use **avoir** in these scenarios.

Expressing Age

Another way that French differs from English is how they express age. Again, they don't say they *are* a certain number of years old. Instead, they say they *have* a certain number of years. This looks like...

I have _____ years. (I am _____ years old)	→ **J'ai** _____ **ans.**
She has _____ years. (She is _____ years old)	→ **Elle a** _____ **ans.**
He has _____ years. (He is _____ years old)	→ **Il a** _____ **ans.**

Even when you're asking for someone's age, keep in mind that you're asking how many years they *have*.

How old are you? *(inf.)*   → Quel âge **as-tu** ?
How old are you? *(form.)* → Quel âge **avez-vous** ?

How old is she? → Quel âge **a-t-elle** ?
How old is he? → Quel âge **a-t-il** ?

How old are they? *(m., co-ed.)* → Quel âge **ont-ils** ?
How old are they? *(f.)*   → Quel âge **ont-elles** ?

Have you noticed that sometimes, you add *a-t-* after 'avoir' ? It's only to help with the pronunciation when the connection between vowels is difficult to make.

Quel âge ont-ils ? Quel âge a-t-il ?

To fill in the blanks above, let's learn some numbers!

Numbers

English	French	Pronunciation
zero	**zéro**	*[zay-roh]*
one	**un**	*[ahn]*
two	**deux**	*[duh]*
three	**trois**	*[trwah]*
four	**quatre**	*[kahtr]*
five	**cinq**	*[sahnk]*
six	**six**	*[sees]*
seven	**sept**	*[set]*
eight	**huit**	*[weet]*
nine	**neuf**	*[neuf]*
ten	**dix**	*[dees]*
eleven	**onze**	*[ohnz]*
twelve	**douze**	*[dooz]*
thirteen	**treize**	*[trayz]*
fourteen	**quatorze**	*[kah-tohrz]*
fifteen	**quinze**	*[kahnz]*
sixteen	**seize**	*[sayz]*
seventeen	**dix-sept**	*[dees-set]*

English	French	Pronunciation
eighteen	**dix-huit**	[dees weet]
nineteen	**dix-neut**	[dees nuff]
twenty	**vingt**	[vahn]
twenty-one	**vingt-et-un**	[vahn tay uh(n)]
twenty-two	**vingt-deux**	[vahn duh]
twenty-three	**vingt-trois**	[vahn twah]
twenty-four	**vingt-quatre**	[vahn kahtr]
twenty-five	**vingt-cinq**	[vahn sank]
twenty-six	**vingt-six**	[vahn seess]
twenty-seven	**vingt-sept**	[vahn set]
twenty-eight	**vingt-huit**	[vahn weet]
twenty-nine	**vingt-neuf**	[vahn nuff]
thirty	**trente**	[trahnt]
thirty-one	**trente-et-un**	[trawnt ay uhn]
thirty-two	**trente-deux**	[trawnt duh]
thirty-three	**trente-trois**	[trawnt twah]
thirty-four	**trente-quatre**	[trawnt katr]
thirty-five	**trente-cinq**	[trawnt sank]
thirty-six	**trente-six**	[trawnt sees]
thirty-seven	**trente-sept**	[trawnt set]
thirty-eight	**trente-huit**	[trawnt weet]
thirty-nine	**trente-neuf**	[trawnt nuff]
forty	**quarante**	[kah-rawnt]

Now that you have a good idea of how the French words for numbers are modified as they increase, let's get a little higher!

English	French	Pronunciation
fifty	**cinquante**	[san-kawnt]
sixty	**soixante**	[swah-sawnt]
seventy	**soixante-dix**	[swah-sawnt-dees]
eighty	**quatre-vingts**	[kat-ruh-van]
ninety	**quatre-vingt-dix**	[kat-ruh-van-dees]
one hundred	**cent**	[sawnt]

English	French	Pronunciation
two hundred	**deux cents**	[duh-sawnt]
three hundred	**trois cents**	[trwah-sawnt]
four hundred	**quatre cents**	[kat-ruh-sawnt]
five hundred	**cinq cents**	[sank-sawnt]
one thousand	**mille**	[meel]
ten thousand	**dix mille**	[dees meel]
one million	**un million**	[uh mee-lyon]
ten million	**dix millions**	[dees mee-lyon]
one billion	**un milliard**	[uh mee-yard]
ten billion	**dix milliards**	[dees mee-yard]
infinity	**infini**	[ahn-fee-nee]

Now let's reinforce this knowledge through some hands-on practice! Are you ready?

Practice 6.2 Age

A. Write the French translations of these English sentences using the correct form of **avoir** to express age.

Example: I'm twenty years old. *J'ai vingt ans.*

1. I'm twenty-five years old. _____
2. I'm thirty years old. _____
3. I'm thirty-seven years old. _____
4. I'm forty-one years old. _____
5. I'm ninety years old. _____

B. Let's make things a little bit harder! Following the same instructions as the prior section, translate these English sentences into French. This time, we're using more than just the first-person singular pronoun.

Example: We are twenty years old. *Nous avons vingt ans.*

1. She is twenty years old. _____
2. We are fifteen years old. _____
3. They (co-ed.) are eighty-five years old. _____
4. They (*f.*) are eighty-six years old. _____
5. You (*inf.*) are twenty-nine years old. _____
6. You (*form.*) are sixty years old. _____
7. I am thirty-eight years old. _____
8. He is one hundred years old. _____

The verb avoir

C. Now, let's combine what you learned about expressing age with the two most important verbs we've learned so far. Read the following French sentences and declare in French whether these people are old (*vieux/vieille*) or young (*jeune*). Remember to match the subject pronoun!

Example: J'ai cent ans. *Je suis vieux.*

1. Elle a deux ans. _____
2. Il a quatre-vingt-dix ans. _____
3. Nous avons dix ans. _____
4. Nous avons quatre-vingt-cinq ans. _____
5. Ils ont quatre-vingt-un ans. _____
6. J'ai huit ans. _____
7. Tu as quatre ans. _____
8. Les femmes ont soixante-dix-neuf ans. _____
9. La fille a onze ans. _____
10. L'homme a quatre-vingt-dix-neuf ans. _____

6.3 Expressing Quantity

As you're aware, we have alternative methods for conveying quantity. Rather than resorting to numerical expressions, opting for terms such as 'a lot' or 'many' provides a nuanced approach. While French offers a plethora of such expressions, we will focus on the most important ones for the moment.

Essential Words Expressing Quantity

English	French	Pronunciation
a lot / many	**beaucoup**	*[boh-koo]*
too much / too many	**trop**	*[troh]*
several	**plusieurs**	*[pluhz-yør]*
a little / a bit	**un peu**	*[ahn pø]*
less	**moins**	*[mwahn]*
more	**plus**	*[pluhs]*

In sentences, this looks like...

He eats a lot.	→ Il mange **beaucoup.**
She has too many cats.	→ Elle a **trop** de chats.
They have too many children.	→ Ils ont **trop** d'enfants.
I have several books.	→ J'ai **plusieurs** livres.
We have a little time.	→ Nous avons **un peu** de temps.
I have more cars than Sally...	→ J'ai **plus** de voitures que Sally...
...but I have less friends than Sally.	→ ... mais j'ai **moins** d'amis que Sally.

Now, let's practice everything you've learned!

Practice 6.3 Quantity

A. Translate these French sentences into English.

1. Marie a dix chats. Elle a trop de chats !

    _____

2. J'ai plus d'enfants que Jennifer.

    _____

3. Il a beaucoup d'oncles et de tantes. Ils sont trop bruyants.

    _____

4. Ils ont un peu d'argent (money).

    _____

5. Nous avons trop de problèmes.

    _____

6. Nina a moins d'amis que Natasha.

    _____

7. James a dix dollars. Jim a quinze dollars. Jim a plus d'argent que James.

    _____

8. Daniel et Emily ont trente euros. Nous avons moins d'argent que Daniel et Emily.

    _____

B. Read the following sentences and indicate in French who has more or less than the other.

Example: Anna has twenty dollars. Abigail has twenty-five dollars. Abigail <u>a plus d'argent qu'Anna</u>.

1. Bill has two cats. Bob has six cats.
    Bill _____.

2. Charlie has three daughters. Chris has five daughters.
    Chris _____.

3. Daniel has fifteen dollars. Daisy has eleven dollars.
    Daisy _____.

4. Emily has thirty books. Eric has sixty-one books.
    Eric _____.

5. I have twelve cars. George has two cars.
    J'ai _____.

C. Read the following French dialogue between two competitive classmates. Answer the questions at the end using the glossary.

ISABELLE : Ma mère a beaucoup d'argent. Elle est très riche.

LUCY : Vraiment ? Mon père aussi a beaucoup d'argent. Il a six voitures.

ISABELLE : Ma mère a plus de voitures que ton père. Elle a neuf voitures.

LUCY : Mon père a un avion.

ISABELLE : Ma mère a deux avions. Nous voyageons beaucoup.

LUCY : Je vais à Paris chaque mois.

ISABELLE : Je vais à Paris chaque semaine !

LUCY : J'achète beaucoup de robes quand je suis à Paris. J'ai deux cents robes.

ISABELLE : J'ai deux mille robes !

LUCY : Tu mens !

ISABELLE : Non, c'est toi qui mens !

Glossary

Vraiment : really?

Un avion : a plane

Nous voyageons : we travel

Je vais : I go

Chaque mois : every month

Chaque semaine : every week

J'achète : I buy

Quand : when

Tu mens : you're lying

1. How many cars does Lucy's father have? _____
    (*Combien de voitures possède le père de Lucy ?*)

2. How many cars does Isabelle's mother have? _____
    (*Combien de voitures possède la mère d'Isabelle ?*)

3. Whose parent has the most planes? _____
    (*Le parent de qui a-t-il le plus d'avions ?*)

4. Who goes to Paris more often? _____
    (*Qui va le plus souvent à Paris ?*)

5. How many dresses does Lucy have? _____
    (*Combien de robes a Lucy ?*)

CHAPTER 7:

FRENCH DEMONSTRATIVES

THERE'S A SMILE ON MY FACE; IT'S A GREAT DAY TO LEARN FRENCH!

7.1 French Demonstratives

Don't be intimidated by the big word! Demonstratives are used to state that something exists. When we say 'There is...' or 'There are...' we are using demonstratives to communicate what is present.

In French, to state 'there is' or 'there are' you begin a sentence with *il y a.* And you'll be relieved to hear that it's the same whether you're talking about a singular noun or a plural noun! It's in the words that follow *il y a* that you indicate whether you're talking about one thing or many things.

For example...

There is a car outside. → **Il y a** une voiture dehors.
There are flowers outside. → **Il y a** des fleurs dehors.

Introduction to Prepositions of Place

To make these demonstratives a little bit more exciting, let's learn some prepositions. Prepositions of place indicate the exact location of something. We'll learn some more later, but for now, let's learn the most important ones.

Essential Prepositions of Place

English	French	Pronunciation
at	à/(au if in front of masculine noun)	[ah]/[oh]
behind	**derrière**	[deh-ryehr]
in/inside	**dans**	[dahn]
in front	**devant**	duh-vahn]
on	**sur**	[sewr]
under	**sous**	[soo]

Here are some example sentences...

She's at the house.	→ **Elle est à la maison.**
There is a cow in the garden.	→ **Il y a une vache dans le jardin.**
The cat is behind the car.	→ **Le chat est derrière la voiture.**
A boy is in front of the house.	→ **Un garçon est devant la maison.**
The book is under the table.	→ **Le livre est sous la table.**
The keys are on the table.	→ **Les clés sont sur la table.**

Now that we have a preliminary understanding of prepositions, it's time to put that knowledge to the test. Are you ready?

Practice 7.1 Demonstratives

A. Translate the following sentences into French using what you just learned about *il y a* and prepositions of place. For now, let's just focus on singular nouns.

1. There's a flower in the garden. _____
2. There's a computer on the table. _____
3. There's a woman in front of the car. _____
4. There's a cat behind the house. _____
5. There's a girl under the table. _____

B. Now, let's bring in some plural nouns and adjectives.

1. There are women in the garden. _____
2. There are keys on the table. _____
3. There are three cats under the car. _____
4. There is a tall man outside. _____
5. There are red and yellow flowers in the garden. _____

7.2 More Demonstratives

We've covered how to say 'there is...' and 'there are...' but what if you want to make a different kind of declaration? Instead of saying 'he is...' or 'she is...' sometimes you want to state that *it* is something.

This is where *c'est* and *ce sont* come in.

Here's how they are used!

It's a beautiful day.	→ **C'est** une belle journée.
It's terrible.	→ **C'est** terrible.
It's a blue sofa.	→ **C'est** un sofa bleu.
It's my mother's car.	→ **C'est** la voiture de ma mère.

And if you're talking about multiple nouns, you use **ce sont**.

They are noisy dogs.	→	**Ce sont** des chiens bruyants.
These are black shoes.	→	**Ce sont** des chaussures noires.
These are red flowers.	→	**Ce sont** des fleurs rouges.
These are my father's socks.	→	**Ce sont** les chaussettes de mon père.

However, in French **c'est** and **ce sont** also work for people.

'She's my mother' can be the same as:

'This is my mother' → C'est ma mère.

'They're my parents' can be the same as:

'These are my parents' → Ce sont mes parents.

Hopefully, you're getting the idea! So, how do you know when to use **c'est** and when to use **il y a**? It's pretty simple. When you're using **c'est**, it's to directly point out something that is right there in front of you. For example, if a plane flies by, you might go, 'It's a plane!' In French this would be: '*C'est un avion !'*

On the other hand, with **il y a** you're simply stating that something exists or that something is happening. However, you're not pointing at it and saying: 'There it is!'

Household Places and Objects

Since we're learning about demonstratives and you now know about prepositions of place, let's learn how to use different places and objects in a house. These words are very helpful when trying to indicate where something is! We've learned some of these words in sentences already, but we'll list them in the following table anyway so you don't forget:

English	French	Pronunciation
Basement	**sous-sol (m.)**	*[soo sohl]*
Bathroom	**salle de bain (f.)**	*[sal duh ban]*
Bedroom	**chambre (f.)**	*[shahm-bruh]*
Dining room	**salle à manger (f.)**	*[sal ah mahn-zhay]*
Garage	**garage (m.)**	*[gah-rahzh]*
Garden	**jardin (m.)**	*[zhar-dan]*
Kitchen	**cuisine (f.)**	*[kwee-zeen]*
Living room	**salon (m.)**	*[sah-lohn]*
Office	**bureau (m.)**	*[byoo-roh]*
Basket	**panier (m.)**	*[pahn-yay]*
Bed	**lit (m.)**	*[lee]*
Car	**voiture (f.)**	*[vwah-tuhr]*

English	French	Pronunciation
Chair	**chaise (f.)**	[shayz]
Door	**porte (f.)**	[pohrt]
Floor	**sol (m.)**	[sohl]
Table	**table (f.)**	[tah-bluh]
Sofa	**sofa/ canapé (m.)**	[soh-fah] / [kah-nah-pay]
Sink	**lavabo (m.)**	[lah-vah-boh]
Shower	**douche (f.)**	[doosh]
Television	**télévision (f.)**	[tay-lay-vee-zyon]
Wall	**mur (m.)**	[myur]
Window	**fenêtre (f.)**	[fuh-netr]

And just like that we are ready for practice! Don't worry, you can also go back in case you don't recall something.

Practice 7.2 Household Vocabulary

A. Translate these French sentences into English using your new household vocabulary words.

1. Les murs sont blancs. _____

2. La maison est petite, mais le jardin est grand. _____

3. J'aime la cuisine. Elle est belle et neuve (new). _____

4. Elle est dans le salon. _____

5. Nous sommes dans le bureau. _____

6. La famille est dans la salle à manger. _____

7. La voiture noire est dans le garage. La voiture rouge est dehors.

    _____

8. La femme est dans la salle de bains. _____

B. Now let's make things even harder using everything we've learned in the book so far.

1. Je suis chauffeur. J'ai trois voitures dans le garage. Une est noire. Deux sont rouges.

    _____

2. Caroline est une fille sympathique. Elle a trente amis et ils sont sympathiques aussi.

    _____

3. Il y a un grand homme dans le garage. C'est mon père. Et la femme sympathique dans la cuisine ? C'est ma mère.

    _____

4. La femme du restaurant est vieille. Elle a quatre-vingt-six ans et elle a huit filles.

    _____

5. Ces chaussures bleues sont neuves. Et ces chaussures vertes sont neuves aussi. J'ai trop de chaussures.

    _____

7.3 The Verb *Aller*

We've covered how to say you *are* and you *have*. Now, it's time to get a little more active. The verb *aller* means 'to go'. It's used to indicate movement, relocation, or your intention to relocate.

Aller *(to go)*			
je	**vais**	nous	**allons**
tu	**vas**	vous	**allez**
il		ils	
elle	**va**	elles	**vont**

Here are some example sentences using **aller.**

I'm going to the museum.	→	**Je vais** au musée.
You're going to school today. (inf.).	→	**Tu vas** à l'école aujourd'hui.
You're going to France with Marie. (form.)	→	**Vous allez** en France avec Marie.
We're going to the supermarket.	→	**Nous allons** au supermarché.
He is going to university.	→	**Il va** à l'université.
She is going to the restaurant with her friend.	→	**Elle va** au restaurant avec son amie.
They are going to the bank. (m., co-ed.)	→	**Ils vont** à la banque.
They are going to work. (f.)	→	**Elles vont** au travail.

> **Tip:** When the place you're referring to is a feminine noun, you say *Je vais à **la banque*** (I'm going to the bank). However, if you're referring to a masculine noun, you say *Je vais **au musée***.

Gear up! Time to put into practice what we have learned!

Practice 7.3 Aller

A. Let's make things harder. Practice **aller** with different subject pronouns, but this time, let's throw some other locations into the mix.

1. _____ au supermarché. *(You are going to the supermarket – inf.)*
2. _____ dans la chambre. *(He's going to the bedroom.)*
3. _____ au bar. *(They are going to the bar – f.)*
4. _____ à la boutique. *(I'm going to the shop.)*
5. _____ au bureau. *(You are going to the office – form.)*
6. _____ au jardin. *(She's going to the garden.)*
7. _____ à la boulangerie. *(They are going to the bakery – co-ed./m.)*
8. _____ au musée. *(We are going to the museum.)*
9. _____ au restaurant. *(You are going to the restaurant – pl.)*
10. _____ à la banque. *(I'm going to the bank.)*

French demonstratives

B. Let's make the sentences even trickier. Translate these French sentences into English.

1. C'est une belle journée. Nous allons au parc.

   _____

2. Le supermarché est derrière la boulangerie.

   _____

3. Je suis dans le jardin et tu vas au travail.

   _____

4. La femme dans la voiture va à la banque.

   _____

5. Emily et Daniel vont au musée avec leurs amis.

   _____

6. Ma mère est à la maison. Mon père va au supermarché.

   _____

7. La famille va au restaurant.

   _____

8. Il va au bar dans sa nouvelle voiture.

   _____

9. Il y a un chien devant le restaurant.

   _____

10. Je vais à la maison ! Il y a une vache dehors.

   _____

Other Ways of Using *Aller*

The verb **aller** is incredibly useful. You can even use it to indicate how you're doing. In English, this would be like if someone asked you, 'How's it going?' and you responded with 'It's going well'.

In French, this looks like...

How's it going?	→	**Comment ça va ?**
Is your mother doing well?	→	**Est-ce que ta mère va bien ?**
Are they doing well?	→	**Vont-ils bien ?**

And you would answer...

It's going well.	→	**Ça va bien.**
She's doing well.	→	**Elle va bien.**
We're doing well.	→	**Nous allons bien.**
They're doing well (co-ed.).	→	**Ils vont bien.**

Time to practice!

Practice 7.4 Correct Sentences

A. Let's see if you can spot whether these French sentences are grammatically correct or not. Pay attention to the conjugations, subject pronouns, articles, and word choices. If the sentence is correct, place a tick next to it. If it's wrong, place an X there instead.

1. _____ Je allons bien.
2. _____ Je vais chez le médecin demain.
3. _____ Ce sont un beau chien.
4. _____ J'aime ces femmes, ils sont belles.
5. _____ Nous allons à l'école demain.
6. _____ Vous avons un examen.
7. _____ Le chien va bien.
8. _____ Les chats sont à la maison.
9. _____ La vache est dans le jardin.
10. _____ Il a médecin.

B. For all the grammatically incorrect sentences in the previous exercise, write the corrections below.

1. _____
2. _____
3. _____
4. _____
5. _____

C. Likewise, let's try to choose the correct word in parentheses. Remember, there's only one right answer!

1. Le chat [va / vont] dans la maison.
2. La voiture [est / sont] dans le garage.
3. Les filles [a / ont] des jolies robes.
4. Vous [a / avez] beaucoup d'argent.
5. Nous [vont / allons] au parc avec Marie.

Speak Abroad
Academy

MORE IMPORTANT VERBS
DO AS I DO

8.1 Present Tense of *Faire*

You're still with me, yeah? Okay good! Let's learn some more important verbs. *Faire* is an incredibly useful verb that allows you to say 'to do' or 'to make'. It's used very often to convey many kinds of expressions. It's also helpful when we're talking about activities and hobbies, like going shopping, exercising, and so on.

Faire *(to do/ to make)*			
je	**fais**	nous	**faisons**
tu	**fas**	vous	**faites**
il		ils	
elle	**fait**	elles	**font**

We can use *faire* in sentences like the following:

I'm making a cake.	→	**Je fais** un gâteau.
I'm shopping.	→	**Je fais** du shopping.
She's cycling.	→	**Elle fait** du vélo.
She does sports.	→	**Elle fait** du sport.
He's doing his homework.	→	**Il fait** ses devoirs.
He's making the bed.	→	**Il fait** le lit.
You're doing the dishes (inf.).	→	**Tu fais** la vaisselle
We do photography.	→	**Nous faisons** de la photographie.
They are exercising (co-ed.).	→	**Ils font** de l'exercice

Buckle up, there's a practice exercise coming up!

Practice 8.1 *Faire*

A. To get used to this new verb, let's practice using different conjugations of *faire* with this sentence about making the bed.

1. _____ le lit. (*You are making the bed – inf.*)
2. _____ le lit. (*I'm making the bed.*)
3. _____ le lit. (*We are making the bed.*)
4. _____ le lit. (*They are making the bed – co-ed.*)
5. _____ le lit. (*He is making the bed.*)
6. _____ le lit. (*They are making the bed – f.*)
7. _____ le lit. (*She is making the bed.*)
8. _____ le lit. (*You are making the bed – form.*)

B. Now, let's work on some slightly more complex sentences using *faire*. Translate the following into English.

1. Nous faisons un gâteau dans la cuisine.

   _____

2. La grande femme fait de l'exercice dans le jardin.

   _____

3. Les deux amis font du sport dans le parc.

   _____

4. L'homme gentil fait la vaisselle.

   _____

5. Emily et Erica sont dans les magasins. Elles font du shopping.

   _____

8.2 Talking About the Weather with *Faire*

As we mentioned earlier, *faire* is a very useful adjective. It's also used to talk about the weather in an impersonal way. We use *faire* because the weather is constantly *doing* something; it's not just one fixed state. Here's how we use *faire* in a sentence to talk about the weather...

The weather is good. → **Il fait beau.**
It's sunny.   → **Il fait soleil.**
The weather is bad. → **Il fait mauvais.**
The weather is cold. → **Il fait froid.**
The weather is hot.   → **Il fait chaud.**

However, we don't use *faire* to describe all kinds of weather. For example...

It's snowing. → **Il neige.**
It's raining. → **Il pleut.**
It's windy.   → **Il y a du vent.**

Speak Abroad
Academy

Weather and Climate Vocabulary

In order to describe the weather better, here are some new vocabulary words. Remember which one's you're supposed to use with *faire*.

English	French	Pronunciation
Weather	**météo (f.)**	[may-tay-oh]
Cold	**froid**	[frwah]
Hot	**très chaud**	[tray show]
Warm	**chaud**	[shoh]
Sun	**soleil**	[soh-lay]
Rain	**pluie (f.)**	[plwee]
Cloud	**nuage (m.)**	[nwee-ahzh]
Snow	**neige (f.)**	[nehzh]
Storm	**tempête (f.)**	[tahm-pet]
Wind	**vent (m.)**	[vahng]
Thunder	**tonnerre (m.)**	[toh-nair]
Lightning	**éclair (m.)**	[ay-klair]
Damp	**humide**	[ew-meed]
Dry	**sec**	[sek]
Wet	**mouillé**	[moo-yay]

Practice 8.2 Weather

A. Let's practice some basic sentences regarding the weather. Read what the following characters are wearing and determine whether it's cold (*il fait froid*), it's hot (*il fait chaud*), or it's raining (*il pleut*).

1. Paula is wearing a raincoat (*Paula porte un manteau imperméable*).

     _____

2. Thomas is wearing a scarf, coat, and gloves (*Thomas porte une écharpe, un manteau et des gants*). _____

3. Marie is wearing a bikini (*Marie porte un bikini*). _____

4. Eddy is using an umbrella (*Eddy utilise un parapluie*). _____

5. Sally is wearing sunglasses and sunscreen (*Sally porte des lunettes de soleil et de la crème solaire*). _____

B. Read the following French descriptions of different weather. Circle the most appropriate clothing to wear in these different climates.

1. Il fait froid et il neige.

A. a coat *(un manteau)*   B. sandals *(des sandales)*   C. a swimsuit *(un maillot)*

2. Il fait beau et il fait chaud.

A. shorts *(short)*   B. an umbrella *(un parapluie)* C. a scarf *(une écharpe)*

3. Il fait mauvais. Il pleut. Il y a du vent, du tonnerre et des éclairs.

A. an umbrella *(un parapluie)* B. a swimsuit *(un maillot)*   C. a short skirt *(une jupe courte)*

8.3 Present Tense of *Vouloir*

Sometimes it's essential to indicate if there's something you want or if you have a strong will for something. That's where the verb *vouloir* comes in. It means 'to want'.

Vouloir *(to want)*			
je	**veux**	nous	**voulons**
tu	**veux**	vous	**voulez**
il		ils	
elle	**veut**	elles	**veulent**

Here's how it's used:

I want a skirt.	→	Je **veux** une jupe.
The little girl wants a dog.	→	La petite fille **veut** un chien.
He wants a croissant.	→	Il **veut** un croissant.
She wants to go to the park.	→	Elle **veut** aller au parc.
We want a new car.	→	Nous **voulons** une nouvelle voiture.
They want a bigger house (co-ed.).	→	Ils **veulent** une maison plus grande.

Practice 8.3 Vouloir

Let's practice using the present tense of *vouloir*. Add the correct conjugations to the following sentences.

1. _____ une nouvelle petite amie. (*You want a new girlfriend – inf.*)
2. _____ aller au musée aujourd'hui. (*I want to go to the museum today.*)
3. _____ faire du shopping. (*She wants to go shopping.*)
4. _____ un hamster. (*We want a hamster.*)
5. _____ avoir plus d'enfants. (*They want to have more children – co-ed.*)

More important verbs

Politeness

In English, it would be considered rude to say 'I want juice' or 'I want coffee' if you go to a restaurant. It's just as off-putting in French. This is why it's best to not use *vouloir*, when you're in these situations. Instead, you should use the...

8.4 Conditional Tense of *Vouloir*

When something is in the conditional tense, it means that the verb's action is not being as strongly conveyed. It sounds a bit more uncertain. In English, this becomes 'would like' instead of 'want'. Saying you 'would like' something is a lot more polite than simply saying you want something.

Vouloir *(would want / would like)*			
je	**voudrais**	nous	**voudrions**
tu	**voudrais**	vous	**voudriez**
il elle	**voudrait**	ils elles	**voudraient**

With this conditional tense, it becomes way more polite to ask for things that you want. For example:

I would like a newspaper.	→	**Je voudrais** un journal.
She would like a coffee.	→	**Elle voudrait** un café.
He would like a dessert.	→	**Il voudrait** un dessert.
We would like a bottle of wine.	→	**Nous voudrions** une bouteille de vin.
They would like a menu *(co-ed.)*.	→	**Ils voudraient** un menu.

Practice 8.4 Conditional *Vouloir*

A. Translate the following sentences into French using what you just learned about the conditional tense of *vouloir*.

1. He would like some flowers.

   _____

2. We would like three coffees, please.

   _____

3. I would like a blue shirt and a white skirt.

   _____

4. They would like a table. *(co-ed.)*

   _____

5. She would like a black coat.

   _____

B. Read the following French dialogue between a mother and her daughter. Then, refer to the glossary provided and answer the following questions.

PAULINE : Nous avons besoin d'un cadeau pour l'anniversaire de Grand-mère.
ANNA : Elle voudrait avoir un nouveau chat.
PAULINE : Elle a quatre chats ! Cinq chats, c'est trop.
ANNA : Bon, d'accord. Elle veut une robe. Une robe rouge ! Et des chaussures blanches aussi.
PAULINE : Une robe rouge pour Mamie ?
ANNA : Oui, il y a un nouveau magasin à côté de la boulangerie. Les vêtements sont si jolis !
PAULINE : Ah ! C'est toi qui veux de nouveaux vêtements. C'est ça, Anna ?

Glossary

Nous avons besoin : We need
Un cadeau : a gift
Anniversaire : birthday
Mamie : Grandma

À côté : next to
Les vêtements : the clothes
C'est toi : it's you
C'est ça ? : Is that right?

1. Whose birthday is it? _____
2. What was Anna's first suggestion? _____
3. Where is the new store located? _____
4. How many cats does Granny have? _____
5. Who actually wants to get new clothes? _____

C. Translate the following French sentences into English using everything you've learned so far.

1. Nous faisons nos courses au supermarché. Les fruits sont chers !

   _____

2. Il fait beau. Il y a des fleurs dans le parc. Je veux aller au parc.

   _____

3. Il fait le lit. Tu fais la vaisselle. Et moi ? Je suis dans un bar avec des amis.

   _____

4. Il pleut. Les nouveaux vêtements sont mouillés.

   _____

5. Il fait froid aujourd'hui ! Je voudrais un café chaud. Elle veut aussi du café.

   _____

8.5 Present Tense of *Porter*

We've used this verb in some exercises in this chapter. *Porter* means 'to wear' or 'to carry'.
It's most commonly used to indicate what clothes you're wearing.

Porter *to wear / to carry*			
je	**porte**	nous	**portons**
tu	**portes**	vous	**portez**
il	**porte**	ils	**portent**
elle		elles	

Here's how it's used in different sentences...

I'm wearing an expensive necklace.	→	**Je porte** un collier cher.
He's wearing an ugly jacket.	→	**Il porte** une veste laide/moche.
She's carrying a heavy bag.	→	**Elle porte** un sac lourd.
We're wearing formal clothes.	→	**Nous portons** des vêtements formels.

You get the idea! Now, it's time to test your knowledge!

Practice 8.5 *Porter*

A. Fill in the blanks with the correct conjugation for each sentence.

1. _____ chaussures chères. (*He's wearing expensive shoes.*)
2. _____ une belle écharpe. (*You're wearing a beautiful scarf – inf.*)
3. _____ la même robe. (*They're wearing the same dress – f.*)
4. _____ des lunettes de soleil dehors. (*She wears sunglasses outside.*)
5. _____ vêtements tous les jours. (*I wear clothes every day.*)

B. Translate the following sentences into English using everything you've learned so far.

1. C'est une belle journée. Je porte une nouvelle chemise et nous allons dans un restaurant cher.

    _____

2. Je porte une veste marron, mais je voudrais une veste noire.

    _____

3. Il fait chaud aujourd'hui. Je porte des lunettes de soleil et un short. Je vais au parc avec des amis.

    _____

4. Elle porte des vêtements chers, mais ces vêtements sont vieux et moches.

    _____

5. Je voudrais quatre petits chapeaux jaunes, s'il vous plaît. Ils sont pour mes chats !

    _____

CHAPTER 9:

EATING AND DRINKING

I EAT THE CHEESE, YOU DRINK THE WINE

9.1 Food & Drink Vocabulary

With all the hard work you've done, you deserve to be rewarded! Therefore, it's time for a fun chapter: food and drink! We've covered some French words for food and drink already, but you can never learn enough words when it comes to eating and drinking. Here are some important words to keep in mind:

English	French	Pronunciation
Bread	pain (m.)	[pah(n)]
Cheese	fromage (m.)	[froh-mahzh]
Ham	jambon (m.)	[zhah(n)-boh(n)]
Sausages	saucisses (f.)	[soh-seess]
Egg	œuf (m.)	[uhf]
Sugar	sucre (m.)	[sookr]
Butter	beurre (m.)	[buhr]
Fish	poisson (m.)	[pwah-soh(n)]
Beef	bœuf (m.)	[buhf]
Chicken	poulet (m.)	[poo-lay]
Vegetables	légumes (m.)	[lay-goom]
Meat	viande (f.)	[vyahnd]
Salad	salade (f.)	[sah-lahd]
Mushroom	champignon (m.)	[shah(n)-pee-nyoh(n)]
Potato	pomme de terre (f.)	[pohm duh tehr]
Chocolate	chocolat (m.)	[shoh-koh-lah]
Ice Cream	glace (f.)	[glahss]
Cake	gâteau (m.)	[gah-toh]
Wine	vin (m.)	[vahn]
Water	eau (f.)	[oh]

English	French	Pronunciation
Milk	**lait (m.)**	*[lay]*
Beer	**bière (f.)**	*[byair]*
Juice	**jus (m.)**	*[zhoo]*
Coffee	**café (m.)**	*[kah-fay]*
Tea	**thé (m.)**	*[tay]*
Hot chocolate	**chocolat chaud (m.)**	*[shoh-koh-lah shoh]*
Fruit	**fruit (m.)**	*[frwee]*
Apple	**pomme (f.)**	*[pohm]*
Orange	**orange (f.)**	*[oh-rahnzh]*
Banana	**banane (f.)**	*[bah-nahn]*
Pear	**poire (f.)**	*[pwahr]*
Cherry	**cerise (f.)**	*[suh-reez]*
Strawberry	**fraise (f.)**	*frez]*
Lemon	**citron (m.)**	*[see-trohn]*
Peach	**pêche (f.)**	*[pesh]*
Meal	**repas (m.)**	*[ruh-pah]*
Breakfast	**petit-déjeuner (m.)**	*[puh-tee day-zhuh-nay]*
Lunch	**déjeuner (m.)**	*[day-zhuh-nay]*
Dinner	**dîner (m.)**	*[dee-nay]*
Dessert	**dessert (m.)**	*[deh-sehr]*

Sometimes you will need to add 'du' (m.) or 'de la (f.) when talking about an unknown or unspecified quantity of something uncountable.

I want (some) sugar. = Je veux **du** sucre.

She'd like some water. = Elle voudrait **de** l'eau (remember you can't have ' de la' in front of a vowel)

You know all fun experiences are incomplete without some practice so here it is!

Time for you to challenge yourself.

Practice 9.1 Food

A. Can you remember what these foods are in English?
1. Du pain et du fromage _____
2. Du poisson et des légumes _____
3. Un café avec du sucre _____
4. Poulet et bœuf _____
5. Un thé avec du lait _____

B. Using what you know about numbers, see if you can identify what these plural food items are.
1. Dix œufs _____
2. Cinq pommes _____
3. Quinze pommes de terre _____
4. Trois bananes _____
5. Trente-cinq citrons _____

C. Translate the following sentences into French using the conditional form of *vouloir*.
1. I would like a coffee with milk and sugar.

    _____

2. We would like meat and vegetables.

    _____

3. He would like a beer and she would like a juice.

    _____

4. She would like mushrooms in the salad.

    _____

5. They would like bread and butter (co-ed.).

    _____

D. Translate these French sentences into English.
1. Elle voudrait de la glace sur le gâteau.

    _____

2. Il voudrait du poisson et des légumes pour le dîner.

    _____

3. Je voudrais une bière avec le dîner.

    _____

4. Je voudrais des fraises et du chocolat.

    _____

5. Ils voudraient des œufs, du jambon et du pain.

    _____

9.2 Conveying Units of Food & Drink

Sometimes it's necessary to describe whether you want a cup of coffee or a pot of coffee. In that case, 'de' is the easiest translation for 'of'. For the rest, the following words will help you be more precise:

English	French	Pronunciation
A cup of...	une tasse de	[uhn tahs duh]
A bottle of...	une bouteille de	[ewn boo-tay duh]
A glass of...	un verre de	[uh(n) vehr duh]
A bowl of...	un bol de	[uh(n) bohl duh]
A plate of...	une assiette de	[ewn ah-syet duh]
A spoonful of...	une cuillerée de	[ewn kwee-ay-ray duh]
A handful of...	une poignée de	[ewn pwa-nyay duh]

Time for a practice test once again!

Practice 9.2 Units of Food

A.   Translate the following French sentences into English using what we've learned so far in this chapter.
1.   Une cuillerée de sucre _____
2.   Une tasse de lait _____
3.   Une poignée de fraises _____
4.   Une assiette de saucisses _____
5.   Une bouteille de vin _____

B.   Let's make the sentences a little more complex.
1.   Il y a une tasse de café sur la table.

_____

2.   Il y a une assiette d'œufs et de jambon dans la cuisine.

_____

3.   Il y a du thé dans la tasse, mais je voudrais un café.

_____

4.   Il y a cinq bouteilles de bière sur la table dans le jardin.

_____

5.   Il y a une bouteille de vin dans la chambre. C'est pour l'anniversaire de Marie.

_____

9.3 Present Tense of *Manger*

Now that you know the French words for various foods and drinks, it's time to introduce the most important verb in this topic. It's the verb *manger*! As I'm sure you can guess, it means 'to eat' and it's extremely useful in everyday life.

Manger *(to eat)*			
je	**mange**	nous	**mangeons**
tu	**manges**	vous	**mangez**
il	**mange**	ils	**mangent**
elle		elles	

Here's how it's used in a sentence...

Every day, I eat a big lunch.	**Chaque jour, je mange un gros déjeuner.**
He eats a lot.	**Il mange beaucoup.**
She eats dessert every evening.	**Elle mange du dessert chaque soir.**
We are eating eggs and sausages for breakfast.	**Nous mangeons des œufs et des saucisses au petit déjeuner.**
You eat like a cow. (inf.)	**Tu manges comme une vache.**
They are eating together. (co-ed.)	**Ils mangent ensemble.**

Have you noticed that 'I eat' and 'they are eating' are both translated by the present tense of 'manger'? Actually, French people use the present tense for activities that take place regularly and actions that are happening right now. It makes things so much easier when you think about it!

Let's do a practice exercise to really solidify that knowledge! Are you with me?

Practice 9.3 *Manger*

A. Fill the blanks with the correct conjugations of *manger*.
1. _____ au restaurant. (*They are eating at the restaurant – f.*)
2. _____ trop bruyamment. (*You are eating too loudly – inf.*)
3. _____ parce que j'ai faim. (*I'm eating because I'm hungry.*)
4. _____ tout le gâteau. (*They are eating all the cake – co-ed.*)
5. _____ encore une salade. (*She is eating a salad again.*)

Speak Abroad
Academy

B. Write the following sentences in French.

1. I'm eating an apple for breakfast.

   _____

2. We are eating a big plate of fish. It's delicious!

   _____

3. They (co-ed.) are eating in the garden tonight.

   _____

4. She's eating a handful of strawberries.

   _____

5. He is eating ice cream for dessert.

   _____

9.4 Present Tense of *Boire*

You know how to say 'to eat,' but how about 'to drink'? That's where *boire* comes in!

Boire *to drink*			
je	**bois**	nous	**portons**
tu	**bois**	vous	**portez**
il	**boit**	ils	**portent**
elle		elles	

Here's how it's used in a sentence...

I drink too much beer.	**Je bois trop de bière.**
He's drinking a glass of orange juice.	**Il boit un verre de jus d'orange.**
She's drinking a bottle of water.	**Elle boit une bouteille d'eau.**
You drink a lot of juice (inf.)	**Tu bois beaucoup de jus.**
We are drinking champagne in the morning.	**Nous buvons du champagne le matin.**
They are drinking wine at the restaurant. (co-ed.)	**Ils boivent du vin au restaurant.**
They are drinking wine at the bar. (f.)	**Elles boivent du vin au bar.**

Now you have the perfect companion for "manger"!

Practice 9.4 *Boire*

A. Let's put your expanded French vocabulary to the test. Translate the following French sentences into English.

1. Chaque soir, il boit trop de bière et je mange trop de gâteau.

   _____

2. Nous sommes au restaurant. Il y a une grande assiette de bœuf sur la table. C'est délicieux !

   _____

3. Pour le petit-déjeuner, je bois du café avec du sucre et du lait. Louis boit un verre de jus de pomme.

   _____

4. Il y a une assiette d'œufs et de saucisses dans la cuisine. C'est pour toi !

   _____

5. Andy et Angela boivent beaucoup de vin. Bob et moi, nous mangeons beaucoup de salade.

   _____

B. Time for a reading comprehension exercise. Read the following passage and answer the questions by referring to the glossary given below.

Au restaurant

Nous sommes dans un restaurant français populaire. Nous sommes huit à table. Nous travaillons ensemble dans le même bureau. La table est très grande. Nous commandons quatre bouteilles de vin et beaucoup de viande. Je mange du bœuf et je bois un verre de vin. Il y a aussi du poulet, du poisson et des légumes. C'est délicieux ! Toute la soirée, nous parlons, rions, mangeons et buvons. Quelle merveilleuse soirée !

Glossary

Populaire : popular
Même : same
Nous commandons : We order
Nous travaillons ensemble : We work together

Toute la soirée : all night
Nous parlons : we talk
Nous rions : we laugh
Merveilleuse : marvelous

1. What type of restaurant are they eating at? _____

2. How many people are at the table? _____

3. What's the relationship between all the people at dinner? _____

4. What do they order to drink? _____

5. Name all the food items that they order for dinner. _____

CHAPTER 10:

LIKES AND DISLIKES
I LIKE LEARNING FRENCH

10.1 The Present Tense of *Aimer*

Now, we can finally start expressing our opinions. With the verb *Aimer*, which means 'to like' or 'to love', you can let others know about all the things that you enjoy. This verb will come in handy when you're getting to know people.

Aimer *(to like / to love)*			
je	**aime**	nous	**aimons**
tu	**aimes**	vous	**aimez**
il	**aime**	ils	**aiment**
elle		elles	

Here's how it's used in a sentence...

I like cows.	→	**J'aime** les vaches.
He likes the color pink.	→	**Il aime** la couleur rose.
She likes her new house.	→	**Elle aime** sa nouvelle maison.
We like French restaurants.	→	**Nous aimons** les restaurants français.
You like this car a lot. (form.)	→	**Vous aimez** beaucoup cette voiture.
You like France. (inf.).	→	**Tu aimes** la France.
They like the blue sofa. (co-ed.)	→	**Ils aiment** le sofa bleu.

> **Tip:** Remember that when you're using *aimer* to talk about yourself, **je** becomes **j'** because the next word begins with a vowel. It's always **j'aime** and never, ever *je aime*!

Let's check your comprehension by introducing a small practice exercise! Are you ready?

Practice 10.1 *Aimer*

Fill in the blanks with the correct form of *aimer* for these simple sentences.

1. Tu _____ les chats.
2. J'_____ le fromage français.
3. Nous _____ les fleurs jaunes.
4. Vous _____ le grand jardin.
5. Il _____ la belle femme.
6. Elle _____ la nouvelle boutique.
7. Ils _____ la voiture chère.
8. Elles _____ la glace.

10.2 Hobbies & Interests Vocabulary

In order to practise using *aimer*, it's helpful to know the French words for common interests and hobbies. Which of the following do you like and enjoy? Can you say it in French using what you just learned about *aimer*?

English	French	Pronunciation
Music	la musique (f.)	[lah myoo-zeek]
Computer Games	les jeux sur ordinateur (m.)	[lay zhuh syur or-dee-nah-tur]
Video Games	les jeux vidéo (m.)	[lay zhuh vee-day-oh]
Board Games	les jeux de société (m.)	[lay zhuh duh so-see-ay-tay]
Photography	la photographie (f.)	[lah foh-toh-grah-fee]
Books	les livres (m.)	[lay leevr]
Fiction Novels	les romans de fiction (m.)	[lay roh-mahn duh feek-syon]
Poetry	la poésie (f.)	[lah pway-zee]
Movies	les films (m.)	[lay feelm]
Art	l'art (m.)	[lahr]
Chess	les échecs (m.)	[lay zay-sheck]
Sports	le sport (m.)	[luh spor]
Basketball	le basketball (m.)	[luh bas-ket-ball]
Soccer	le football (m.)	[luh foot-ball]
Tennis	le tennis (m.)	[luh teh-nees]

Practice 10.2 Hobbies

Using what you learned above, write the following sentences in French.

1. We like music a lot. _____
2. I like fiction novels. _____
3. They (co-ed.) like photography. _____
4. He likes board games. _____
5. You like art a lot. _____

Additional Verbs

Occasionally, you might wish to express the actions involved in pursuing your hobbies. The table below introduces various verbs commonly associated with the aforementioned hobbies (poetry, music, board games) or can be used independently.

English	French	Pronunciation
To listen to	**écouter**	*[ay-koo-tay]*
To play	**jouer**	*[zhoo-ay]*
To write	**écrire**	*[ayk-reer]*
To watch	**regarder**	*[ruh-gahr-day]*
To read	**lire**	*[leer]*
To cook	**cuisiner**	*[kwee-zee-nay]*
To draw	**dessiner**	*[day-see-nay]*
To dance	**danser**	*[dahn-say]*
To paint	**peindre**	*[pahndr]*

Here are some examples of how to use the above verbs with the new vocabulary you've learned so far.

I like to listen to music.	→	**J'aime écouter de la musique.**
She likes to play video games.	→	**Elle aime jouer aux jeux vidéo.**
He likes to play basketball.	→	**Il aime jouer au basketball.**
We like to write novels.	→	**Nous aimons écrire des romans.**
You like to watch TV (form.).	→	**Vous aimez regarder la télévision.**
You like to read (inf.).	→	**Tu aimes lire.**
They like to cook (co-ed.).	→	**Ils aiment cuisiner.**
They like to dance together (f.).	→	**Elles aiment danser ensemble.**

> **Tip:** By the way, just like in English, where we say 'I like to DO something, in French you need to keep the infinitive form of the second verb
>
> I like to go to the park = J'aime aller au parc, not J'aime vais au parc.

10.3 Using *Faire* with Hobbies

We learned *faire* which means 'to do' or 'to make' in an earlier chapter. It comes in handy when you're talking about certain hobbies. For example:

English	French	Pronunciation
Baking	**(faire de) la pâtisserie (f.)**	*[fair duh la pah-tee-SEE-ree]*
Hiking	**(faire de) la randonnée (f.)**	*[fair duh la ran-doh-NAY]*
Biking/ cycling	**(faire du) vélo (m.)**	*[fair dew vay-LOH]*
Gardening	**(faire du) jardinage (m.)**	*[fair dew zhar-dee-NAHZH]*
Exercising/ working out	**(faire de) l'entraînement (m.)**	*[fair duh lon-tray-NAH-mahn]*
Sailing	**(faire de) la voile (f.)**	*[fair duh la VWAL]*
Shopping	**(faire du) shopping (m.)**	*[fair dew SHOP-ing]*

Attempt the following practice exercise to really solidify your understanding.

In situations like these, you can't have 'de le' in front of a masculine word. Instead, you need to use 'du'.

Practice 10.3 *Faire* + hobbies

A. Write the following sentences in French.
   1. He likes to play chess. _____
   2. She likes to bake. _____
   3. They (co-ed.) like to play video games. _____
   4. I like to play board games. _____
   5. You (inf.) like to listen to music and I like to dance. _____

B. Translate the following sentences into English.
   1. Ils aiment jouer ensemble dans le jardin.

   _____

   2. Elle aime faire du sport à l'école.

   _____

   3. Nous aimons écouter de la musique le matin.

   _____

   4. Il aime manger des gâteaux. J'aime faire des gâteaux.

   _____

   5. J'aime regarder la télévision avec mon ami.

   _____

6. Elles aiment faire du shopping à Paris.

   _____

7. Tu aimes faire du jardinage.

   _____

8. Vous aimez lire des livres intéressants.

   _____

C. Let's make these sentences more complex and combine everything we've learned so far. Translate these sentences into English.

   1. Il a une télévision parce qu'il aime les films. (parce que = because)

      _____

   2. Rachel aime la viande. Elle voudrait une assiette de poulet, s'il vous plaît.

      _____

   3. J'aime jouer au foot avec le chien blanc.

      _____

   4. Nous aimons jouer aux jeux vidéo avec des belles femmes.

      _____

   5. Elles aiment les fleurs. Tous les jours, ils aiment jardiner ensemble.

      _____

10.4 Expressing Your Dislikes

For the first time in this book, we'll begin constructing a negative sentence. Using the same verb, *aimer*, and the same conjugations, you can also express that you don't like something. The following affirmative sentences become negative sentences like this...

I don't like to listen to music.	→	**Je n'aime pas** écouter de la musique.
She doesn't like to play video games.	→	**Elle n'aime pas** jouer aux jeux vidéo.
He doesn't like to play basketball.	→	**Il n'aime pas** jouer au basketball.
We don't like to write novels.	→	**Nous n'aimons pas** écrire des romans.
You don't like to watch TV (form.).	→	**Vous n'aimez pas** regarder la télévision.
You don't like to read (inf.).	→	**Tu n'aimes pas** lire.
They don't like to cook (co-ed.).	→	**Ils n'aiment pas** cuisiner.
They don't like to dance together (f.).	→	**Elles n'aiment pas** danser ensemble.

> **Tip:** In order to use *aimer* in a negative sentence, you add **n'** in front of the *aimer* conjugation and then add **pas** after it. Since **n** is a consonant and not a vowel, this also means that **j'** turns back into **je**. So **j'aime** becomes **je n'aime pas**.

Try the following practice exercise to really solidify your understanding.

Practice 10.4 Dislikes

A. Let's get used to saying you 'don't like' something with *aimer*. Turn these affirmative sentences from an earlier exercise into negative sentences.
   1. _____ les chats. (*You don't like cats – inf.*)
   2. _____ le fromage français.(*I don't like French cheese.*)
   3. _____ les fleurs jaunes.(*We don't like yellow flowers.*)
   4. _____ la nouvelle boutique. (*She doesn't like the new shop.*)
   5. _____ la voiture chère. (*They don't like the expensive car – co-ed.*)

B. Turn the following affirmative sentences into negative sentences.
   1. J'aime les musées. _____
   2. Elle aime les chats noirs. _____
   3. Nous aimons le vin. _____
   4. Ils aiment manger dans des restaurants chers. _____
   5. Vous aimez regarder la télévision. _____
   6. Ils aiment manger de la glace. _____
   7. Vous aimez jouer au tennis. _____
   8. Il aime lire dans le jardin. _____

C. Turn the following negative sentences into affirmative sentences.
   1. Ils n'aiment pas cuisiner. _____
   2. Il n'aime pas porter des chaussures. _____
   3. Elle n'aime pas boire de la bière. _____
   4. Ils n'aiment pas manger du fromage. _____
   5. Nous n'aimons pas regarder la télévision le soir. _____

D. Translate these English sentences into French.
   1. He wants a big garden. He likes to garden.

   _____

   2. She eats a lot, but she doesn't like vegetables.

   _____

   3. I like the color yellow. I don't like the color black.

   _____

   4. We like the bread at the bakery. We don't like the bread at the restaurant.

   _____

   5. They don't like to watch TV together.

   _____

CHAPTER 11:

NEGATION
I DON'T DANCE

11.1 Constructing Negative Sentences with *Ne... pas*

In the previous chapter, you learned how to construct a negative French sentence by saying you 'do not like' something. As you know, this is not the only type of negative sentence that exists. In fact, every single verb can be used negatively. For example, you can say 'I go' and 'I don't go' or 'I have' and 'I don't have'.

An affirmative sentence would be 'the cat is blue'. In retort to this, a negative sentence would be 'the cat is not blue'.

To make a sentence negative, you add the words **ne... pas**, with the verb in the sentence. If the verb begins with a vowel, it becomes **n'... pas.** This is the equivalent of adding 'do not' to a sentence.

Here are some examples:

I like cats.	→	I don't like cats.
J'aime les chats.	→	**Je n'aime pas les chats.**
I am a cat.	→	I'm not a cat.
Je suis un chat.	→	**Je ne suis pas un chat.**
I'm going to the church.	→	I'm not going to the church.
Je vais à l'église.	→	**Je ne vais pas à l'**église.
You are happy (inf.).	→	You are not happy.
Tu es heureux.	→	**Tu n'es pas heureux.**
We want a new car.	→	We don't want a new car.
Nous voulons une nouvelle voiture.	→	**Nous ne voulons pas de nouvelle voiture.**
They have a daughter (co-ed.).	→	They don't have a daughter.
Ils ont une fille.	→	**Ils n'ont pas de fille.**

It's important to know that when there's an indefinite article (un/une) or a partitive article (du/de la/des) used to mean 'some' after a negative, the article can often change to 'de' or 'd".

She eats meat.	→	She doesn't eat meat.
Elle mange de la viande.	→	**Elle ne mange pas de viande.**
He drinks beer.	→	He does not drink beer.
Il boit de la bière.	→	**Il ne boit pas de bière.**
He has some new books.	→	He does not have any new books.
Il a des nouveaux livres.	→	**Il n'a pas de nouveaux livres.**

Practice 11.1 *Ne... pas*

A. Let's practice turning affirmative sentences into negative sentences. For now, let's stick to the first-person singular pronoun.

1. Je suis une vache. _____
2. Je mange un gâteau. _____
3. Je vais à la gare. _____
4. J'ai un gentil frère. _____
5. Je veux un nouveau chat. _____
6. Je voudrais un bol de cerises. _____
7. Je porte un chapeau bleu. _____
8. J'aime les fleurs. _____
9. Je bois un verre de vin. _____
10. J'ai quarante ans. _____

B. Now, let's bring in the other subject pronouns. Turn these following sentences into negative sentences.

1. Vous aimez le parapluie jaune. _____
2. Il veut un verre d'eau. _____
3. Elle va manger. _____
4. Elles portent de nouveaux vêtements. _____
5. Nous buvons beaucoup de jus d'orange. _____
6. Ils sont des hommes riches. _____
7. Elle est triste. _____
8. Nous avons deux fils. _____
9. Vous allez à l'école. _____
10. Tu travailles beaucoup. _____

C. Write the following negative sentences in French.

1. She doesn't want the small house. _____
2. I don't want to read a book. _____
3. We don't eat meat. _____
4. They *(co-ed.)* don't have a white cat. _____
5. I am not a doctor. _____

D. Which of the following negative sentences are grammatically incorrect?

1. _____ Je mange pas de viande.
2. _____ Je ne sors pas de la maison.
3. _____ Je ne suis pas content.
4. _____ Nous ne voulons jouer.
5. _____ Vous n'aimez pas l'école.
6. _____ Ils sont pas grands.

E. Correct the incorrect sentences in the prior exercise.

1. _____
2. _____
3. _____

11.2 Constructing Negative Sentences with Ne... jamais

Sometimes it isn't enough to say you aren't doing something; sometimes it's necessary to say you *never* do something. That's where **ne... jamais** comes in. This indicates that the verb is never performed.

She never listens.	→ **Elle n'écoute jamais.**
I never go outside.	→ **Je ne sors jamais.**
He never eats vegetables.	→ **Il ne mange jamais de légumes.**
They never have money *(co-ed.)*.	→ **Ils n'ont jamais d'argent.**
We never drink orange juice.	→ **Nous ne buvons jamais de jus d'orange.**

You get the idea!

Practice 11.2 Ne... jamais

A. Turn these affirmative sentences into negative sentences using **ne... jamais**.

1. Elle a de l'argent. _____
2. Le grand homme va au supermarché. _____
3. Je mange de la viande. _____
4. Nous allons à l'école. _____
5. Ils prennent le petit-déjeuner ensemble. _____
6. Vous buvez de la bière. _____
7. Elles font le lit. _____
8. Tu vas à l'église. _____

B. Which of the following negative sentences are grammatically incorrect?
    1. Il travaille jamais.
    2. Elle ne m'écoute jamais.
    3. Je ne sors de la maison.
    4. Nous ne mangeons jamais ensemble.
    5. Vous ne aimez pas cuisiner avec moi.
    6. Tu ne vas jamais au théâtre.

C. Correct the incorrect sentences in the prior exercise.
    1. _____
    2. _____
    3. _____

D. Read the following short French passage and answer the questions using the glossary provided. Can you understand what the speaker is complaining about?

Mon fils a deux ans. Ce n'est pas un garçon calme, il est bruyant. Il ne mange jamais ses légumes et il ne range jamais ses affaires. Nous n'allons jamais au restaurant, parce qu'il est très vilain. Je suis fatigué. J'ai besoin de vacances !

Glossary:

Garçon calme : quiet boy
Bruyant : noisy
Toujours : always
Ranger ses affaires : tidy up his things

Vilain : naughty
Fatigué : tired
J'ai besoin : I need
Vacances : a vacation

    1. How old is the speaker's son? _____
    2. Is the son quiet or noisy? _____
    3. What does he never eat? _____
    4. Where does the speaker never take his son? _____
    5. What does the speaker need? _____

E. Translate the following French sentences into English.
    1. Elle n'aime pas manger de dessert. Elle mange des salades.

        _____

    2. J'ai cinq enfants ; je ne vais jamais au cinéma !

        _____

    3. Il aime aller dans des restaurants chers, mais il n'a jamais d'argent.

        _____

    4. Tu aimes la poésie triste. Tu n'es jamais heureux !

        _____

    5. Nous ne buvons jamais de bière. Nous voudrions avoir deux verres de vin.

        _____

ASKING QUESTIONS
DO YOU LIKE FRENCH?

12.1 Asking Questions with *Est-ce que...*

So far, you've practiced making a lot of statements. But what about asking questions? Just like English, there are many ways to ask questions in French. It all depends on what type of information you're looking for.

The most basic way to ask a question is by beginning a sentence with **est-ce que...** (pronounced 'ess keu') This can turn any statement into a yes or no question. It translates to 'is it that..?' which is understood more commonly in English as 'is it so that..?'

> Tip: *Est-ce que* becomes *est-ce qu'* in front of a vowel: **Do they? → Est-ce qu'ils ?**

Let's see how this works!

You like apples.	→	Do you like apples?
Tu aimes les pommes.	→	**Est-ce que tu aimes les pommes ?**
She has a big house.	→	Does she have a big house?
Elle a une grande maison.	→	**Est-ce qu'elle a une grande maison ?**
He is going to the office.	→	Is he going to the office?
Il va au bureau.	→	**Est-ce qu'il va au bureau ?**
They want to go to the museum.	→	Do they want to go to the museum?
Ils veulent aller au musée.	→	**Est-ce qu'ils veulent aller au musée ?**
I am a cow.	→	Am I a cow?
Je suis une vache.	→	**Est-ce que je suis une vache ?**

The following practice exercise will help you test your understanding.

Practice 12.1 *Est-ce que*

A. Turn the following statements into questions using ***est-ce que*** following the examples listed above.

1. Nous aimons la voiture orange. _____

2. Elle va à la gare. _____

3. Ils sont jeunes. _____

4. Nous avons une belle voiture. _____

5. Jenny a plus d'argent que James. _____

B. The following statements are answers to specific questions. Write the French questions that they are answering.

Example: Oui, il est prêt. Est-ce qu'il est prêt ? *(Yes, he's ready. Is he ready?)*

1. Non, je n'aime pas les chiens. _____

2. Oui, c'est un vieil homme. _____

3. Oui, ils vont au restaurant français. _____

4. Non, nous ne sommes pas riches. _____

5. Non, ils ne vont pas aller à la boulangerie. _____

12.2 Asking Questions with Inversions

Inverted questions tend to be more common, specifically in more formal situations. When a question is inverted, the verb goes before the subject pronoun and it's connected by a hyphen. Like this...

Aimes-tu les pommes ? *(Do you like apples?)*
A-t-elle une grande maison ? *(Does she have a big house?)*
Va-t-il au bureau ? *(Is he going to the office?)*
Veulent-ils aller au musée ? *(Do they want to go to the museum?)*
Suis-je une vache ? *(Am I a cow?)*
Es-tu content ? *(Are you happy?)*

Ready to practice?

Practice 12.2 Inversions

A. Turn the following statements into questions using inversions following the examples listed above.

1. Tu as une voiture.

2. Il boit du vin.

3. Nous aimons le nouveau restaurant.

4. Elle fait du sport.

5. Elles aiment jouer au football.

B.   Change the following questions with ***est-ce que*** into inverted questions.

    1.   Est-ce que vous faites toujours du sport les week-ends ?

    2.   Est-ce que je dois finir mon examen ce matin ?

    3.   Est-ce qu'elle est contente de venir ici ?

    4.   Est-ce qu'il va au bureau le samedi ?

    5.   Est-ce que tu es content de regarder ce film avec moi ?

12.3 Who, What, Where...

Without English words like who, what, or where, it would be extremely difficult to ask certain questions. Of course, there are others too like when, how, and why, but for now, let's focus on these three.

In French, the equivalents of these words are:

who	**qui**	*[kee]*
what*	**quoi / que / quel / quelle**	*[KWAH]/ [KUH]/ [KEL]/ [KEL]*
where	**où**	*[oo]*

We can ask questions with them like this:

English	French + Pronunciation	Example
who	**qui** *[kee]*	**Who is the woman in the black dress?** → Qui est la femme avec la robe noire ? **Who is your best friend?** → Qui est ton meilleur ami ?
what*	**quoi / que / quel / quelle** *[KWAH]/ [KUH]/ [KEL]/ [KEL]*	**What does he want?** → Que veut-il ? **What day is it?** → Quel jour sommes-nous **?**
where	**où** *[oo]*	**Where is the new restaurant?** → Où est le nouveau restaurant ? **Where is the cat?** → Où est le chat ?

*A Note on 'What'

There are a few different words that replace *'what'* in French. Not every word is appropriate for every type of sentence. Through practice you'll get used to each word and when it's best to use it.

Here's a few common examples for you:

What time is it? → **Quelle heure est-il ?**

How old is she? → **Quel âge a-t-elle ?**

What is your favorite movie? → **Quel est ton film préféré ?**

What are you eating tonight? → **Que mangez-vous ce soir ?**

Practice 12.3 Who, What, Where

Answer the following questions in French using the clues given to you.

*Note : *'Where is'* can be translated by **Où est** or **Où se trouve**.

1. Où se trouve votre école ?
    _____ (est/ mon école/ l'église/ devant)
2. Qui est l'homme avec le chapeau noir ?
    _____(mon père/ c'est)
3. Quelle est ta couleur préférée ?
    _____(le violet/ est/ ma couleur préférée)
4. Qui est ta femme ?
    _____(est/ écrivaine/ ma femme)
5. Où se trouve le vieux musée ?
    _____(à côté du/ il est/ nouveau restaurant)

12.4 When, How, Why

Now it's time for the next set of important interrogative words! These question allies add depth and curiosity to your expressions, allowing you to navigate the intricacies of time, manner, and reason.

when	**quand**	*[koh~]*
how	**comment**	*[koh-moh~]*
why	**pourquoi**	*[poor-kwah]*

We can ask questions with them like this:

Quand arrive-t-elle ? *(When does she arrive?)*
Quand est la fête ? *(When is the party?)*

Comment vas-tu ? *(How are you doing?)*
Comment sait-elle quand le film commence ? *(How does she know when the movie starts?)*

Pourquoi es-tu triste ? *(Why are you sad?)*
Pourquoi as-tu un parapluie ? *(Why do you have an umbrella?)*

Attempt the following questions to test your understanding. Are you ready?

Practice 12.4 When, How, Why

Answer the following questions in French using the clues given to you. For now, let's just focus on 'when' and 'how.'

1. Quand le concert commence-t-il ? (ce soir/il commence)

   _____

2. Comment va votre mari ? (très bien/ mon mari/ va)

   _____

3. Quand vient-elle ? (venir/ elle va/ ce soir)

   _____

4. Quand est-ce que vous buvez du vin ? (au restaurant/ français/ nous allons/ quand)

   _____

5. Comment va ton frère ? (ne va pas/ mon frère/ bien)

   _____

12.5 Answering *Pourquoi*

In English, the word 'because' is crucial to provide a correct answer to the question 'why?' In French, there's an equivalent for this. In spoken French, it's generally expressed as **parce que**, while in written French, **car** is more common. For now, we'll concentrate on the former to emphasize improving spoken French.

Whenever the word following it begins with a vowel, it is shortened to **parce qu'** and joined to the next word.

This is how to construct a proper answer to *pourquoi*:

J'ai un parapluie parce qu'il pleut. *(I have an umbrella because it's raining.)*
Il mange parce qu'il a faim. *(He's eating because he's hungry.)*
Je suis heureux parce que c'est une bonne journée.
(I'm happy because it's a good day.)

Nous sommes riches parce que nous avons beaucoup de vaches.
(We are rich because we have many cows.)
Elle porte un manteau parce qu'elle a froid.
(She wears a coat because she's cold.)
Ils dansent parce qu'ils sont heureux. *(They are dancing because they're happy.)*

Practice 12.5 Pourquoi

Translate the following French sentences into English.

1. J'ai un chat parce que j'aime les chats.

   _____

2. Il est dehors parce qu'il n'aime pas le chien.

   _____

3. Tu portes un short parce qu'il fait très chaud.

   _____

4. Nous jouons beaucoup aux échecs parce que nous sommes intelligents.

   _____

5. Tu manges cinq bols de glace parce que tu es triste.

   _____

12.6 Combining Common French Expressions with Prepositions

Here are some common expressions where these words are combined with prepositions to have a whole different meaning.

English	French	Pronunciation
With whom?	**avec qui**	[ah-VEK kee]
For whom?	**pour qui**	[poor kee]
About whom?	**à propos de qui**	[ah proh-POH duh kee]
To whom? Who for?	**pour qui**	[poor kee]
At whose place?	**chez qui**	[shay kee]
With what?	**avec quoi**	[ah-VEK kwah]
From where?	**d'où**	[doo]
Which one?	**lequel/ laquelle**	[luh-KEL]/ [lah-KEL]

Here are some example sentences:

D'où viens-tu ? *(Where do you come from?)*
Tu préfères laquelle ? *(talking about a shirt – Which one do you like?)*
Pour qui est cette vache ? *(Who is this cow for?)*

Practice 12.6 French Expressions with Prepositions

A. Can you translate these French questions into English?
1. Avec qui Jacob va-t-il au restaurant ? _____
2. Elle veut une veste ? Laquelle ? _____
3. Pour qui fais-je un gâteau ? _____
4. Chez qui es-tu ? _____
5. D'où viennent-elles ? _____

B. Read the following French dialogue and then answer the questions, which are written in French. Use the glossary provided for reference.

TOM : Il y a une fête ce soir. Tu y vas ?
BEN : Oui. J'y vais avec quelqu'un.
TOM : Avec qui ?
BEN : Sasha. La femme qui travaille à la boulangerie. Et toi ?
TOM : J'y vais seul. Que vas-tu porter ?
BEN : Une chemise noire et un jean. Où est la fête ?
TOM : C'est au bar de Max.
BEN : C'est le bar avec les fleurs devant ou celui à côté de la station service ?
TOM : C'est le bar derrière l'église.
BEN : OK, à bientôt !

Glossary:

A party : une fête   Alone : seul
Tonight : ce soir   She works : elle travaille
Someone : quelqu'un   See you soon : à bientôt
Gas station : station service

1. Avec qui Ben va-t-il à la fête ? _____
2. Où travaille la femme ? _____
3. Que porte Ben ? _____
4. Où est le bar ? _____
5. C'est le bar de qui ? _____

CHAPTER 13:

TIME, DATES, AND SEASONS
IT'S TIME TO LEARN FRENCH!

13.1 Asking For & Expressing the Time

Navigating everyday life would be pretty hard without the ability to express the time. But before we can say what time it is, let's learn how to ask for the time!

There are actually many different ways to ask for the time in French. Not all of them are appropriate in every situation, since some will depend on formality. When you're around friends, family, and people you use informal language with, you can ask for the time by saying...

Quelle heure est-il ?
Il est quelle heure ?
C'est à quelle heure ? *(What time is it at?)* – For specific events

When you're addressing people you don't know well or anyone you use formal language with, you could ask for the time using the above questions, but you should better use...

Puis-je avoir l'heure s'il vous plaît ?
Quelle heure est-il, je vous prie ?

Yet, the most common way of asking for the time in French is...

Quelle heure est-il ?

Asking for the Time of Specific Events

Sometimes it isn't enough to just ask what time it is now. If you're waiting for a specific event, you'll also want to ask what time something takes place. You can construct these questions like this...

À quelle heure est la fête ? *(What time is the party?)*
À quelle heure est le rendez-vous ? *(What time is the appointment?)*
À quelle heure est le dîner ? *(What time is dinner?)*

And to answer you would say...

La fête est à 20h. *(The party is at 8pm.)*
Le rendez-vous est à 9h. *(The appointment is at 9am.)*
Le dîner est à 19h. *(Dinner is at 7pm.)*

Expressing the Time in French

Now that you know how to ask for the time, let's learn how to answer the question. The numbers you learned in an earlier chapter come in very handy here! If someone asks you what time it is and it's 2 p.m. in the afternoon, you should answer:

Il est quatorze heures

You may notice that the number up there is actually fourteen – not two. This is because it's customary in France to use military time. In other words, a 24-hour clock. This means that 1 p.m. becomes **treize heures**, 2 p.m. becomes **quatorze heures**, and so on.

But it is also quite common to simply say : **il est deux heures (de l'après-midi).**

If there are minutes involved, you could say : **il est quatorze heures et vingt minutes.**

But French people would most likely tell you : **il est deux heures vingt/il est quatorze heures vingt.**

Let's get those neurons firing by doing some practice exercises!

Time Vocabulary

Just like in English, there are easier ways of telling the time. If it's 8:15 in the morning, you may want to say 'quarter past eight' instead of 'eight fifteen'. To simplify the expressions of time, the following words will be very useful:

English	French	Pronunciation
Morning	matin (m.)	[ma-TAN]
Afternoon	après-midi (m.)	[ah-PRAY mee-DEE]
Noon	midi (m.)	[mee-DEE]
Evening	soir (m.)	[SWAR]
Night	nuit (f.)	[NWEE]
Midnight	minuit (m.)	[mee-NWEE]
Half past...	et demi	[ay duh-MEE]
Quarter to...	moins le quart	[mwan luh KAR]
Quarter past...	et quart	[ay KAR]
After	après	[ah-PRAY]
Almost	presque	[PRESK]
Hour	heure (f.)	[UR]
Minute	minute (f.)	[mee-NOOT]
Second	seconde (f.)	[suh-GOND]

They can be used like this:

It's quarter to two. → **Il est deux heures moins le quart.**
It's quarter past two. → **Il est deux heures et quart.**
It's half past eight. → **Il est huit heures et demie.**

It's noon. → **Il est midi.**
It's almost midnight. → **Il est presque minuit.**
It's one in the morning. → **Il est une heure du matin.**

> **Tip:** The official rule is that these fractions (**et quart, et demi**...) are informal and only work with a 12-hour clock. When in doubt, it's usually better to say **il est huit heures et quart** than **il est vingt heures et quart**.
>
> To clearly avoid confusion between 8 a.m. or 8 p.m. without an obvious context, you simply need to mention '**du matin**' or '**du soir**':
>
> **He comes at 8 a.m.** → Il vient à 8 heures du matin.
>
> **He finishes work at 8 p.m.** → Il finit le travail à 8h du soir.

However, you might still hear fractions with a 24-hour clock when you're at the station or the airport:

Le train pour Paris part à 13h55 (treize heures cinquante-cinq)
(The train for Paris leaves at 13:55.)

Practice 13.1

A. Read the following sentences. When they're not grammatically correct, mark them with an X.
1. _____ Puis-je avoir l'heure s'il vous plaît ?
2. _____ Il heure quelle est ?
3. _____ Quelle heure est-il, je vous prie ?
4. _____ À c'est heure quelle ?

B. Ask for the time of the following events in French.
1. Le film (*The movie*) _____
2. Le concert (*The concert*) _____
3. La fête d'anniversaire (*The birthday party*) _____
4. La classe d'art (*The art class*) _____
5. Le pique-nique (*The picnic*) _____

C. Say what time it is in English using a 12-hour clock and a.m. or p.m.
   1. Il est treize heures _____
   2. Il est huit heures vingt _____
   3. Il est vingt-trois heures quinze _____
   4. Il est sept heures trente _____
   5. Il est dix-huit heures et trente-trois minutes _____

D. State what the time is in French using the 24-hour clock.
   1. 10:40 a.m. _____
   2. 6:10 a.m. _____
   3. 3:05 p.m. _____
   4. 7:50 p.m. _____
   5. 11:18 p.m. _____

E. Using what you've learned about expressing time so far, write in French what the following times are.
   1. 9:00 a.m. _____
   2. 10:30 a.m. _____
   3. 12:00 p.m. _____
   4. 1:15 p.m. _____
   5. 1:45 p.m. _____
   6. 4:30 p.m. _____
   7. 7:45 p.m. _____
   8. 10:15 p.m. _____

13.2 Expressing the Date

When making plans or looking at a schedule, it's vital to know the words for the days of the weeks, the months, and other ways of measuring longer stretches of time.

English	French	Pronunciation
Monday	**lundi**	*[lun-DEE]*
Tuesday	**mardi**	*[mar-DEE]*
Wednesday	**mercredi**	*[mehr-kruh-DEE]*
Thursday	**jeudi**	*[zhuh-DEE]*
Friday	**vendredi**	*[vahn-druh-DEE]*
Saturday	**samedi**	*[sam-DEE]*
Sunday	**dimanche**	*[dee-MAHNSH]*

English	French	Pronunciation
January	**janvier**	*[zhahn-VYAY]*
February	**février**	*[fay-VRYAY]*
March	**mars**	*[MARHS]*
April	**avril**	*[ah-VREEL]*
May	**mai**	*[MAY]*
June	**juin**	*[zhwaN]*
July	**juillet**	*[zhwee-YAY]*
August	**août**	*[OOT]*
September	**septembre**	*[sep-TAHMb]*
October	**octobre**	*[awk-TOBR]*
November	**novembre**	*[noh-VAHMb]*
December	**décembre**	*[day-SAHMb]*
Yesterday	**hier**	*[YER]*
Today	**aujourd'hui**	*[oh-zhoor-DWEE]*
Tomorrow	**demain**	*[duh-MAN]*
Day	**jour**	*[ZHOOR]*
Week	**semaine**	*[suh-MEN]*
Month	**mois**	*[MWAH]*
Year	**an**	*[AHN]*
Next...	**prochain**	*[proh-SHAN]*
Last...	**dernier**	*[der-NYAY]*

'An' works better for a duration or a specific year:

for 10 years   → **pendant 10 ans**
in the year 2023 → **en l'an 2023**

But if you're talking about last year or next year, it's better to use 'année' instead:

last year   → **l'année dernière**
next year   → **l'année prochaine**

Here are some examples of how to express the date using these words...

It's Monday.   → **C'est lundi.**
Tomorrow is Tuesday.   → **Demain c'est mardi.**
The party is next month. → **La fête est le mois prochain.**
It's July next month.   → **Le mois prochain est juillet.**
She arrives in January.   → **Elle arrive en janvier.**

It's Friday today.	→	**C'est vendredi aujourd'hui.**
Is it Saturday today?	→	**Est-ce que c'est samedi aujourd'hui ?**
On Monday, we eat steak.	→	**Le lundi, nous mangeons du steak.**
We celebrate Christmas in December.	→	**Nous célébrons Noël en décembre.**

Practice 13.2

A. Let's test your memory of the new vocabulary you've learned.

1.   October _____
2.   February _____
3.   June _____
4.   April _____
5.   August _____
6.   July _____
7.   Wednesday _____
8.   Friday _____
9.   Tuesday _____
10. Saturday _____
11. Yesterday _____
12. Tomorrow _____
13. Today _____
14. Next month _____

B. Write the following sentences in French.

1.   It's Thursday today. _____
2.   It's November next month. _____
3.   He arrives in March. _____
4.   The concert is next week. _____
5.   On Saturday, we go to the park. _____

Seasons

Let's learn the French words for the seasons. These go hand-in-hand with what you've learned about dates. Take a look at the table below and delve into the linguistic tapestry as you uncover the French vocabulary for the seasons.

English	French	Pronunciation
Spring	**printemps (m.)**	[prahn-toh~]
Summer	**été (m.)**	[ay-tay]
Autumn / fall	**automne (m.)**	[oh-tohm-nə]
Winter	**hiver (m.)**	[ee-vayr]

Here's how we can use these words:

C'est **l'hiver**. *(It's winter.)*
L'été **dernier**. *(Last summer.)*
Au **printemps**, je fais du vélo. *(In spring, I go cycling.)*
En **été**, j'aime jouer au football. *(In summer, I like to play football.)*
En **hiver**, elle porte un manteau. *(In winter, she wears a coat.)*
En **automne**, nous buvons du chocolat chaud. *(In autumn, we drink hot chocolate.)*

> **Tip:** To say what day it is, what month, which season, or even which year, just add 'on est' at the beginning. It's a bit casual, but it's a lifesaver in many situations!
>
> On est lundi.
>
> On est en janvier.
>
> On est au printemps.
>
> On est en 2023.

Now let's do some practice exercises to really test that knowledge!

C. For the following months, state whether **c'est l'hiver, l'été, l'automne** ou **le printemps**.

1. Octobre _____
2. Août _____
3. Décembre _____
4. Mai _____

13.3 Frequency

Here are some other words that come in handy when talking about time and the frequency of events:

English	French	Pronunciation
Sometimes	**parfois**	*[par-FWAH]*
Often	**souvent**	*[soo-VAHN]*
Every day / each day	**chaque jour**	*[SHAK zhoor]*
Every night / each night	**chaque nuit**	*[SHAK nwee]*
Every week / each week	**chaque semaine**	*[SHAK suh-MEN]*
Every/ each...	**chaque**	*[SHAK]*
Once a day	**une fois par jour**	*[ewn FWAH par zhoor]*
Twice a day	**deux fois par jour**	*[duh FWAH par zhoor]*
Once a week	**une fois par semaine**	*[ewn FWAH par suh-MEN]*
Twice a week	**deux fois par semaine**	*[duh FWAH par suh-MEN]*
Once a month	**une fois par mois**	*[ewn FWAH par mwah]*

English	French	Pronunciation
Twice a month	**deux fois par mois**	*[duh FWAH par mwah]*
Once a year	**une fois par an**	*[ewn FWAH par ahn]*
Twice a year	**deux fois par an**	*[duh FWAH par ahn]*

Here's how we can use these words:

Sometimes I eat fish. → **Parfois je mange du poisson.**
She goes to the museum often. → **Elle va souvent au musée.**
Each evening, I drink a glass of wine. → **Chaque soir, je bois un verre de vin.**
We go to Paris once a year. → **Nous allons à Paris une fois par an.**

Now that you've mastered the art of time, dates, and seasons in French, let's put your knowledge to the test!

Are you ready for the challenge?

Practice 13.3

A. Write the following sentences in French.

1. Sometimes I eat a bowl of strawberries.

    _____

2. They go to the park often *(co-ed.)*.

    _____

3. Is it winter? I want a cup of hot chocolate!

    _____

4. It's evening! The party is at 7 PM.

    _____

5. Every morning, we eat a big breakfast together.

    _____

B. Translate the following French sentences into English using everything you've learned so far.

1. Chaque dimanche, il va à la boulangerie et mange un croissant.

    _____

2. Chaque été, nous allons à la plage (the beach). Il fait chaud en août !

    _____

3. On est en avril. Au printemps, j'aime lire dans le jardin.

    _____

4. En hiver, tu portes un élégant manteau noir. Tu es magnifique !

    _____

5. Il est midi et j'ai soif. Chaque après-midi, je bois un grand verre d'eau.

    _____

CHAPTER 14:

MORE ESSENTIALS
YOU AND I, HER OR HIM

14.1 Present Tense of *Parler*

As you continue to enhance your French communication skills, let me introduce you to the versatile verb *parler*. Unsurprisingly, it translates to both 'to speak' and 'to talk'. Get ready to weave this essential thread into the fabric of your growing language proficiency!

Parler *(to speak / to talk)*			
je	**parle**	nous	**parlons**
tu	**parles**	vous	**parlez**
il	**parle**	ils	**parlent**
elle		elles	

Here's how we use it in a sentence...

Oui, **je parle** français. *(Yes, I speak French.)*
Chaque matin, **elle parle** à la vache. *(Each morning, she talks to the cow.)*
Il parle très bien français. *(He speaks French very well.)*
Nous parlons aux fleurs. *(We talk to the flowers.)*
Ils parlent de photographie. *(They are talking about photography. – co-ed.)*
Elles parlent d'art. *(They are talking about art – f.)*
Tu parles comme un pirate. *(You talk like a pirate – inf.)*
Vous parlez français comme un natif. *(You speak French like a native – form.)*

Practice 14.1 *Parler*

A. Let's practice the different conjugations of **parler** with the words for different languages.

1. _____ français. *(I speak French.)*
2. _____ italien. *(You speak Italian – inf.)*
3. _____ espagnol. *(You speak Spanish – form.)*
4. _____ chinois. *(We speak Chinese.)*
5. _____ japonais. *(She speaks Japanese.)*
6. _____ anglais. *(He speaks English.)*
7. _____ allemand. *(They speak German – co-ed.m.)*
8. _____ portugais. *(They speak Portuguese – f.)*

B. Write the following sentences in French using everything you've learned so far.

1. We talk together every week.

    _____

2. They talk to Alex once a month *(co-ed.)*.

    _____

3. Sometimes they speak Spanish *(f.)*.

    _____

4. The intelligent man speaks French very well.

    _____

5. Each morning, you talk to the baby (inf.).

    _____

6. I don't speak Spanish.

    _____

7. She talks a lot.

    _____

8. Why do you talk to the cow?

    _____

C. Translate the following sentences into English.

1. J'aime parler à ma grand-mère. Elle est très drôle et intéressante.

    _____

2. Je parle à Jane toutes les semaines parce que nous sommes de bonnes amies.

    _____

3. Pourquoi parles-tu au chat ? Le chat ne parle pas anglais !

    _____

4. Qui parle ? Est-ce Emma et Esther ? Elles parlent trop.

    _____

5. Il parle aux chiens parce qu'il aime les animaux.

    _____

14.2 Conjunctions & Prepositions

Don't be intimidated by that big word! Conjunctions are some of the most common parts of everyday language. They connect other words, phrases, and clauses. For example, in that last sentence, 'and' was the conjunction, because it unites the rest of the sentence.

Some other examples of conjunctions are 'or' and 'but'. They allow us to say things like 'She came by, but she didn't come in'.

We've used some of these already, but it's time to learn even more! Consider the table below and then attempt the practice exercise:

English	French	Pronunciation
And	**et**	[ay]
Or	**ou**	[oo]
But	**mais**	[may]
If	**si**	[see]
So	**alors/donc**	[ah-lohr]
As / since / like a	**comme**	[kohm]
then	**puis**	[pwee]

Practice 14.2 Conjunctions

A. Let's start off simple. Fill in the blanks with the correct conjunction, either **et**, **ou**, or **mais**.

1. Le garçon aime les fruits. Il mange une banane _____ une pomme.
2. Est-ce que Martin est médecin _____ avocat ?
3. Je veux cette robe, _____ elle est chère.
4. Est-ce que vous arrivez à huit heures _____ neuf heures ?
5. Il veut la voiture rouge, _____ sa femme aime la voiture rose.

B. Circle or underline the correct conjunction in the following sentences.

1. Il va à l'église, [mais / puis / ou] il va au bar.
2. La voiture est rouge [et / alors / comme] une tomate.
3. Elle est triste [comme / donc / ou] elle mange beaucoup de glace.
4. Je voudrais une grande bouteille de vin [si / et / mais] nous allons au restaurant.
5. Le garçon est grand [comme / ou / puis] mon père.

14.3 More Prepositions

Let's learn the French words for some very useful time prepositions. These go hand-in-hand with what you've learned about dates and expressing the time.

English	French	Pronunciation
During / while	**pendant**	[pahn-DAHN]
After	**après**	[ah-PRAY]
Before	**avant**	[ah-VAHN]
Except	**sauf**	[SOHF]
Until	**jusqu'à**	[zhew-SKAH]

English	French	Pronunciation
With	**avec**	[ah-VEK]
Without	**sans**	[SAHN]
For	**pour**	[POOR]

Practice 14.3 Prepositions

A. Choose the most appropriate preposition for the following sentences.
1. [Sauf / Après / Sans] le dîner, nous regardons la télévision ensemble.
2. Elle fait du sport [avec / sans / jusqu'à] ce soir.
3. Il aime la nourriture [avant / après / sauf] le fromage.
4. Nous buvons une tasse de café [avec / sauf / avant] d'aller au parc.
5. Ils parlent [sans / sauf / pendant] qu'ils font le jardinage.

B. Translate the following sentences into English.
1. Je vais à l'école tous les jours sauf le dimanche.

   _____

2. Il joue au football jusqu'à midi.

   _____

3. Vous mangez et buvez pendant un concert important.

   _____

4. Ils vont au musée avec une vieille femme.

   _____

5. Nous n'aimons pas manger avant de faire du sport.

   _____

C. Convert the following sentences in French.
1. We eat dessert after dinner.

   _____

2. I'm making a cake without sugar.

   _____

3. They are talking during the movie (co-ed.).

   _____

4. She likes to read before breakfast.

   _____

5. He's drinking wine with an interesting man.

   _____

CHAPTER 15:

POSSESSIVES & REFLEXIVES
YOU AND I, HER OR HIM

15.1 Possessive Adjectives

As you know, an adjective describes a noun. When the adjective is possessive, it describes who the noun belongs to and how. It's the difference between saying 'the cat' and '*my* cat' or '*your* cat'. Take a look at the table below for the French words for these possessive adjectives. For now, we'll focus on describing singular nouns.

My	**mon** (m.)	**ma** (f.)
Your	**ton**	**ta**
His / her / its	**son**	**sa**
Our	**notre**	
Your (form.)	**votre**	
Their	**leur**	

This is how we would use them in a sentence...

This is my mother.	→	**C'est ma mère.**
She is your sister.	→	**C'est ta soeur.**
He talks to his cat.	→	**Il parle** à son chat.
Our car is old.	→	**Notre voiture est vieille.**
Alice and Amy, is this your father?	→	**Alice et Amy, est-ce que c'est votre père?**
Their new house is beautiful.	→	**Leur nouvelle maison est jolie.**

Watch out for this tricky part of French grammar! In front of feminine singular nouns beginning with a vowel (and most words beginning with 'h'), *ma* changes to *mon*, *ta* to *ton*, and *sa* to *son*. Why? It just makes it easier to say them in French.

my friend (m.)	→	**mon ami**
my friend (f.)	→	**mon amie**

Plural Possessive Adjectives

Whenever you're referring to multiple nouns, it's essential to use plural possessive adjectives. Thankfully, these are a little easier to use than singular possessive adjectives since the same word is used for both feminine and masculine nouns. Please consider the table below:

My	**mes**
Your	**tes**
His / her / its	**ses**
Our	**nos**
Your (pl. + form.)	**vos**
Their	**leurs**

This is how we would use them in a sentence...

These are my dogs.	→	**Ce sont mes chiens.**
Her sisters are very kind.	→	**Ses sœurs sont très gentilles.**
His cars are expensive.	→	**Ses voitures sont chères.**
Our daughters are young.	→	**Nos filles sont jeunes.**
Their apples aren't ripe.	→	**Leurs pommes ne sont pas mûres.**

> **Tip:** Possessive adjectives must match the noun being possessed in gender and number, not the possessor. What happens if you're referring to your books? You say **mes livres**, even if there's only one of you. And if the person with the books is your friend? It's **ses livres**, even if there's one person holding the books.

You get the idea! Now we must test you!

Practice 15.1

A. Practice using possessive adjectives by converting the following into French.

1. Her book _____
2. My dog _____
3. Our black car _____
4. Your (*inf.*) office _____
5. His glass of wine _____

B. Let's make these sentences a little more complex.

1. Their father is my doctor. _____

2. Her jacket is red and my jacket is white. _____

3. He doesn't talk to his mother. _____

4. Your *(pl.)* son plays football with our son. _____

5. My sister likes to eat at your restaurant. _____

C. Convert the following from singular possessive to plural possessive.

Example: Mon chien. <u>Mes chiens.</u>

1. Ma fleur. _____

2. Son manteau. _____

3. Leur voiture. _____

4. Notre fromage. _____

5. Votre canapé. _____

D. Using everything you've learned about possessive adjectives, translate the following into French.

1. My sister doesn't like your sister.

    _____

2. Where are your brothers?

    _____

3. Your cats are in my garden.

    _____

4. The intelligent woman is their lawyer.

    _____

5. Sometimes our daughters go to the park together.

    _____

15.2 Reflexive Pronouns & Verbs

When you use reflexive verbs, you're indicating that the subject performs an action to themselves. We call it 'reflexive' because it reflects back to the person performing the action. It's the difference between washing a plate and washing *yourself*.

In English, reflexive traits are indicated with words like *myself, yourself, herself, himself, itself, oneself, ourselves, themselves*.

In French, they are indicated by joining a reflexive pronoun to a verb. Reflexive pronouns are words like the following:

Myself	**me**
Yourself	**te**
Himself / herself / itself	**se**
Ourselves	**nous**
Yourselves	**vous**
Themselves	**se**

Don't forget to write **m'**, **t'** or **s'** if the following word starts with a vowel or **h**.

Here's how they work in French sentences.

I wash myself.	→	**Je me lave.**
She washes herself.	→	**Elle se lave.**
He washes himself.	→	**Il se lave.**
We wash ourselves.	→	**Nous nous lavons.**
You wash yourself.	→	**Tu te laves.**
You wash yourselves.	→	**Vous vous lavez.**
They wash themselves (co-ed./m.).	→	**Ils se lavent.**
They wash themselves (f.).	→	**Elles se lavent.**

Yes, you're right! *Nous nous lavons* and *Vous vous lavez* sound a bit strange because of the repetition, but this is the right way to use reflexive French pronouns. Quirky, but accurate.

Reflexive Verbs

Here are some basic reflexive verbs that will come in handy! Remember to replace **se** with the appropriate reflexive pronoun when you're using them in a sentence!

English	French	Pronunciation
To wake oneself	**se réveiller**	*[sə ray-vay-ay]*
To get up	**se lever**	*[sə lə-vay]*
To brush one's teeth	**se brosser les dents**	*[sə broh-say lay doh~]*
To wash oneself	**se laver**	*[sə lah-vay]*
To shower oneself	**se doucher**	*[sə doo-shay]*
To shave oneself	**se raser**	*[sə rah-zay]*
To dress oneself	**s'habiller**	*[sah-bee-yay]*
To undress oneself	**se déshabiller**	*[sə day-zah-bee-yay]*

English	French	Pronunciation
To prepare oneself	**se préparer**	[sə pray-pah-ray]
To look at oneself	**se regarder**	[sə rə-gahr-day]
To ready oneself	**se préparer**	[sə pray-pah-ray]
To calm oneself	se **calmer**	[sə kahl-may]
To hide oneself	se **cacher**	[sə kah-shay]
To rest	**se reposer**	[sə rə-poh-zay]

Practice 15.2

A. Fill in the blanks with the correct subject pronoun and reflexive pronoun.

1. _____ habille. *(I get dressed – 'I dress myself'.)*
2. _____ lève. *(She wakes up – 'She wakes herself'.)*
3. _____ rase. *(He shaves himself.)*
4. _____ douchons. *(We shower ourselves.)*
5. _____ préparent. *(They get ready – 'They ready themselves' – f.)*
6. _____ regardes. *(You look at yourself – inf.)*
7. _____ calmez. *(You calm yourselves.)*
8. _____ cachent. *(They hide themselves – co-ed.)*

B. Read the following passage and answer the questions.

Une journée typique (A typical day)

Chaque matin, Paul se réveille à huit heures. Il se lève à huit heures et quart et se brosse les dents, puis il se douche. Il se rase et s'habille. Après le petit-déjeuner, il va au bureau.

1. What time does Paul wake up? _____
2. How long after waking up does Paul get up? _____
3. What's the first thing Paul does after getting up? _____
4. What does Paul do right after he showers? _____
5. What does he do after he shaves? _____

C. Using the new reflexive verbs you just learned, convert the following into French.

1. He undresses himself. _____
2. I prepare myself. _____
3. They *(f.)* look at themselves. _____
4. They *(m.)* shave themselves. _____
5. You *(inf.)* calm yourself. _____
6. We wake up. _____
7. She dresses herself. _____
8. You *(form./pl.)* rest yourselves. _____

Speak Abroad
Academy

15.3 Present Tense of *Pouvoir*

To fully prepare you for your French journey, here's one more important French verb. *Pouvoir* means 'to be able to' or in other words, 'can'. It's an apt verb to learn in this final section, since you are becoming *able to* speak French!

Pouvoir *(to be able to / can)*			
je	**peux**	nous	**pouvons**
tu	**peux**	vous	**pouvez**
il	**peut**	ils	**peuvent**
elle		elles	

We generally put *pouvoir* in front of other verbs to express that one *can* do something. For example...

Je peux aller à la fête ce soir. *(I can go to the party tonight.)*
Elle peut boire beaucoup. *(She can drink a lot.)*
Vous pouvez venir avec moi. *(You can come with me. – form./pl.)*
Nous pouvons faire un délicieux gâteau. *(We can bake a delicious cake.)*
Elles peuvent être nos amies. *(They can be our friends. – f.)*
Il peut jouer au football comme un professionnel.
(He can play football like a professional.)
Tu peux te réveiller dans l'après-midi. *(You can wake up in the afternoon. – inf.)*
Ils peuvent manger beaucoup de fromage. *(They can eat a lot of cheese. – co-ed, m.)*

Practice 15.3

A. Let's practice different conjugations of **pouvoir**.

1. _____ manger ta tomate. (You can *eat your tomato – inf.*)
2. _____ y aller quand je veux. (I can *go there whenever I want.*)
3. _____ dîner avec nous. (They can *have dinner with us – f.*)
4. _____ avoir nos vieilles chaussures. (They can *have our old shoes – co-ed.*)
5. _____ boire toute la bouteille de vin. (You can *drink the whole bottle of wine – form./pl.*)
6. _____ porter des chapeaux roses à la fête. (We can *wear pink hats to the party.*)
7. _____ avoir la vache. (She can *have the cow.*)
8. _____ jouer aux jeux vidéo chez nous. (He can *play video games at our house.*)

B. Now, let's practice saying 'cannot' with **pouvoir.** Convert the following affirmative sentences into negative sentences.

Example: Je peux marcher. <u>Je ne peux pas marcher.</u>

1. Je peux aller au musée. _____

2. Tu peux manger du fromage. _____

3. Elle peut prendre (*to take*) le croissant. _____

4. Il peut parler à la vache. _____

5. Vous pouvez préparer le petit-déjeuner. _____

6. Nous pouvons manger dans le jardin. _____

7. Ils peuvent parler français. _____

8. Ils peuvent porter des chaussettes à la plage. _____

C. Let's practice everything you've learned so far. Write the following sentences in French.

1. It's Sunday today. There are two men in front of my house. They are my friends. We are going to the museum together.

   _____

2. At 5 PM, I get ready for the party. I'm wearing a beautiful black dress and white shoes.

   _____

3. For dessert tonight, we have cake. Do you want ice cream on the cake?

   _____

4. My brother likes poetry and my sister likes tennis. And me? I like our cat.

   _____

5. In the spring, they (m.) go to the park. In the summer, they (m.) go to the beach. It's too hot, so I go to church.

   _____

Possessives & reflexives

SECTION II:
WORDS & PHRASES

This section will introduce you to some of the most commonly used words and phrases in the French language. We'll give you the tools you need to deal with the most common situations in the various scenarios you might face while living in a French-speaking country. Our plan is for you to quickly scan the book, locate the chapter that corresponds to your needs, and find the phrase you're looking for. While doing so, you will gain an understanding of an important aspect of French culture, which is one of our primary goals with this book.

CHAPTER 16

EVERYDAY ESSENTIALS

In the first chapter, we will provide you with phrases, questions, and answers that are encountered frequently in everyday life. This represents the essentials that all beginners need and you will notice throughout this chapter the importance of courtesy and politeness in French culture.

Whenever possible, we decided to include the written translation in French for both masculine and feminine genders. If you've already studied the lessons in the Workbook, you should already be familiar with them. However, for the sake of brevity, only the masculine pronunciation is explained. Don't worry, it usually doesn't change much at all.

Conversation essentials

This represents the most basic sentences that you might hear or need in France or any French-speaking country:

In the Workbook, you've noticed that there are slight differences between you (informal) and you (formal / group of people).

But here's a quick reminder
You = Tu (informal) or T' (in front of a vowel)
You = Vous (formal/group)

Your = Ta/Ton/Tes
Your = Votre/Vos

Please = **s'il te plaît/s'il vous plaît**

Also verb endings will also change accordingly
You speak   =   Tu parles/Vous parlez
Could you   =   Pourrais-tu/ Pourriez-vous
Are you   =   Es-tu/Êtes-vous

In this book, we'll show you the most casual way to speak in French. Just remember to make the few necessary changes if you have to.

English	French	Pronunciation
Hi	**Salut**	*[sa-LOO]*
Hello	**Bonjour**	*[bon-ZHOOR]*
Nice to meet you	**Enchanté de faire ta connaissance**	*[on-shon-TAY duh FEHR ta koh-nay-SAHNS]*
How was your day?	**Comment s'est passée ta journée ?**	*[koh-MON say pah-SAY ta zhoor-NAY]*

English	French	Pronunciation
My day is going great	**Ma journée se passe très bien**	*[mah zhoor-NAY suh PASS tray byahn]*
I'm having a rough day	**J'ai une journée difficile**	*[zhay oon zhoor-NAY dee-fee-SEEL]*
See you later	**À plus tard**	*[ah PLOOS tar]*
Goodbye	**Au revoir**	*[oh ruh-VWAR]*
Do you speak English?	**Est-ce que tu parles anglais ?**	*[es kuh tyoo parl ahn-GLAY]*
I cannot speak English	**Je ne parle pas anglais**	*[zhuh nuh parl pah ahn-GLAY]*
I can speak English fluently	**Je parle couramment anglais**	*[zhuh parl koo-rah-MON ahn-GLAY]*
I know a bit of English	**Je parle un peu anglais**	*[zhuh PARL uhn puh ahn-GLAY]*
Can you please say that in English?	**Pourrais-tu dire ça en anglais s'il te plaît?**	*[poo-RAY tu deer sah ahn ahn-GLAY seel tuh PLEH]*
I know a bit of French	**Je connais un peu de français**	*[zhuh koh-NAY uhn puh duh frahn-SAY]*
How can I say that in French?	**Comment pourrais-je dire ça en français ?**	*[koh-MAHN poo-RAY zhuh deer sah ahn frahn-SAY]*
I don't understand your question	**Je ne comprends pas ta question**	*[zhuh nuh kohm-PRAHN pah tah kess-TYAWN]*
Can you please repeat that?	**Pourrais-tu répéter s'il te plait?**	*[poo-RAY tu ray-PAY-tay seel tuh PLEH]*
I cannot hear you	**Je ne t'entends pas**	*[zhuh nuh tahn-TAHN pah]*
I am just kidding	**Je plaisante**	*[zhuh pleh-ZAHNT]*
That's very interesting	**C'est très intéressant**	*[say TRAY an-tay-ray-SAHN]*
That's very impressive	**C'est très impressionnant**	*[say TRAY ahn-press-YOH-nahn]*
Excuse me	**Excuse-moi / Pardon**	*[ex-KYOOZ mwah] / [par-DOHN]*
Please	**S'il te plaît**	*[seel tuh PLEH]*
Thank you	**Merci**	*[mehr-SEE]*
Thank you very much	**Merci beaucoup**	*[mehr-SEE boh-KOO]*
You're welcome	**De rien**	*[duh RYANG]*
I am sorry	**Je suis désolé**	*[zhuh SWEE day-zoh-LAY]*
Go ahead	**Vas-y**	*[vah-ZEE]*
Yes	**Oui**	*[WEE]*
No	**Non**	*[NOHN]*
I don't know	**Je ne sais pas**	*[zhuh nuh say PAH]*

English	French	Pronunciation
I don't understand	**Je ne comprends pas**	*[zhuh nuh kohm-PRAHN pah]*
Mister/Sir	**Monsieur**	*[muh-SYEUH] /*
Miss	**Mademoiselle**	*[mad-mwah-ZELL] /*
Mrs	**Madame**	*[mah-DAM]*

Talking about the weather

In France, summers tend to be mild and winters tend to be cool. To enjoy the warmth and sunshine the most, you should go to the beaches in the south of the country. These are the sentences you'll need when talking about the weather in a French-speaking country:

English	French	Pronunciation
What's the weather like today?	**Quel temps fait-il aujourd'hui ?**	*[KEL tawn fay-TEEL oh-zhoor-DWEE]*
What will the weather be like tomorrow?	**Quel temps fera-t-il demain ?**	*[KEL tawn fer-AH-teel duh-MAN]*
It's very hot today	**Il fait très chaud aujourd'hui**	*[EEL fay TRAY sho oh-zhoor-DWEE]*
Will it rain tomorrow?	**Va-t-il pleuvoir demain ?**	*[VAH-teel plew-VWAHR duh-MAN]*
This is a beautiful day	**C'est une belle journée**	*[SAY tune BELL zhoor-NAY]*
It's raining most of next week	**Il pleuvra presque toute la semaine prochaine**	*[EEL plew-VRAH PRESS-kuh toot lah suh-MEN proh-SHEN]*
Rainy	**Pluvieux**	*[plew-VYEU]*
Sunny	**Ensoleillé**	*[awn-so-lay-YAY]*
It is snowing	**Il neige**	*[EEL nezh]*
It's windy	**Il y a du vent**	*[EEL yah dew VAHN]*
Lightning	**Un éclair**	*[uhn ay-KLAIR]*
Thunder	**Le tonnerre**	*[luh toh-NAIR]*
Storm	**Un orage**	*[uhn oh-RAHZH]*
It's cold today	**Il fait froid aujourd'hui**	*[EEL fay FRWAH oh-zhoor-DWEE]*
Look at the rainbow	**Regarde l'arc-en-ciel**	*[ruh-GARD lark-awn-SYEL]*
The wind is blowing	**Le vent souffle**	*[luh VAHN SOO-fluh]*
What's the weather forecast for today?	**Quelle est la météo pour aujourd'hui ?**	*[KEL ay lah may-TAY-oh poor oh-zhoor-DWEE]*

Speak Abroad
Academy

English	French	Pronunciation
It will be misty all morning	**Il y aura de la brume toute la matinée**	*[EEL yoh-RAH duh lah BREWM toot lah mah-tee-NAY]*
It is a heat wave	**C'est une canicule**	*[SAY tune kah-nee-KOOL]*
There are clear skies tonight	**Le ciel est dégagé ce soir**	*[luh SYEL ay day-gah-ZHAY suh SWAR]*

Compliments & showing gratitude

In French culture, politeness and courtesy are emphasized greatly. That's why it's crucial to master the ways of complimenting and showing gratitude, as that's what's going to be expected of you by French people. These are the main sentences and words you'll need:

English	French	Pronunciation
You have a beautiful home	**Tu as une belle maison**	*[tu AH oon bell meh-ZOHN]*
You've been a great host	**Tu as été un hôte formidable**	*[tu AH ay-TAY ün OHT for-mee-DAH-bluh]*
Thank you for this delicious meal	**Merci pour ce délicieux repas**	*[mehr-SEE poor suh day-lee-SYEU re-PAH]*
Thank you for organizing this wonderful event	**Merci d'avoir organisé ce merveilleux événement**	*[mehr-SEE dah-VWAR or-GAH-nee-ZAY suh mehr-VAY-yeuh eh-vay-nuh-MAHN]*
Thank you for inviting me	**Merci de m'avoir invité**	*[mehr-SEE duh mah-VWAR an-vee-TAY]*
I appreciate your concern	**J'apprécie ta sollicitude**	*[zhah-pray-SEE tah so-lee-see-TUHD]*
Thank you for your help/ assistance	**Merci pour ton aide/ assistance**	*[mehr-SEE poor ton ED / ah-see-STAHNS]*
Thank you for being a great friend	**Merci d'être un ami formidable**	*[mehr-SEE DET-ruh ün ah-MEE for-mee-DAH-bluh]*
Thank you for the hospitality	**Merci pour l'accueil**	*[mehr-SEE poor lah-KUH-yuh]*
I am really grateful for this	**Je t'en suis vraiment reconnaissant**	*[zhuh tahn SWEE vray-MAHN ruh-ko-nay-SAHN]*
You're doing a great job	**Tu fais un excellent travail**	*[tu FAY ün ek-say-LAHN trah-VYE]*
This is fantastic	**C'est fantastique**	*[say fahn-TAHS-teek]*
I owe you one	**Je t'en dois une**	*[zhuh tahn DWAH ün]*
I like it	**Ça me plaît**	*[sah muh PLAY]*

CHAPTER 17

BUILDING CONNECTIONS

The beauty of learning a new language is mainly the fact that it allows you to build new connections and maintain relationships with people from other cultures. That's what we aim to help you achieve throughout this chapter.

Introductions

Introductions serve the fundamental purpose of familiarizing individuals with oneself or others, establishing an initial connection, and providing context for ensuing interactions or conversations. The main introductory questions and common responses you need to know when starting introductions with a French-speaking person.

English	French	Pronunciation
What's your name?	**Comment tu t'appelles ?**	*[koh-MOHN tew tah-PELL]*
My name is ___	**Je m'appelle ___**	*[zhuh mah-PELL ___]*
Where are you from?	**D'où viens-tu ?**	*[doo vyahn-TEW]*
I'm from ___	**Je viens de ___**	*[zhuh vyahn duh ___]*
Who are you?	**Qui es-tu ?**	*[kee eh-TEW]*
This is my friend	**Voici mon ami(e)**	*[vwah-SEE moh-nah-MEE]*
This is my husband / wife	**Voici mon mari / ma femme**	*[vwah-SEE moh MAH-ree / mah FAHM]*
This is my father / mother	**Voici mon père / ma mère**	*[vwah-SEE moh PEHR / mah MEHR]*
How old are you?	**Quel âge as-tu ?**	*[kel AHZH ah-TEW]*
I am ___ years old	**J'ai ___ ans**	*[zhay ___ AHN]*
I live in ___	**J'habite à ___**	*[zhah-BEET ah ___]*
We live in ___	**Nous habitons à ___**	*[noo zah-bee-TON ah ___]*
I'm single	**Je suis célibataire**	*[zhuh SWEE say-lee-bah-TAIR]*
I'm married	**Je suis marié**	*[zhuh SWEE mah-REE-AY]*
I'm divorced	**Je suis divorcé**	*[zhuh SWEE dee-vohr-SAY]*
Do you have any siblings?	**As-tu des frères et sœurs?**	*[ah-TEW day FREHR ay SUHR]*
I have ___ brothers	**J'ai ___ frères**	*[zhay ___ FREHR]*
I have ___ sisters	**J'ai ___ soeurs**	*[zhay ___ SUHR]*

English	French	Pronunciation
I'm an only child	**Je suis enfant unique**	*[zhuh SWEE ahn-FAHN ew-NEEK]*
Do you have a big family?	**As-tu une grande famille?**	*[ah-TEW ew-n GRAHND fah-MEE]*
Do you live alone?	**Vis-tu seul ?**	*[vee-TEW SUHL]*
Do you have any pets?	**As-tu des animaux domestiques?**	*[ah-TEW day zah-nee-MOH doh-mehs-TEEK]*

Work & Professions

This is how to ask and answer questions regarding work and professions in French as well as a list of the most common professions in French.

English	French	Pronunciation
What do you do for a living?	**Que fais-tu dans la vie ?**	*[Kuh fay TU da(n) lah VEE]*
Where do you work?	**Où travailles-tu ?**	*[OO trah-VY TU]*
I work from home	**Je travaille à domicile**	*[Zhuh trah-VY ah doh-MEE-seel]*
I work freelance	**Je travaille en freelance**	*[Zhuh trah-VY ahn FREE-lah(n)s]*
I work a lot	**Je travaille beaucoup**	*[Zhuh trah-VY BOH-koo]*
I don't work on the weekends	**Je ne travaille pas le week-end**	*[Zhuh nuh trah-VY pah luh WEE-kehnd]*
I am unemployed	**Je suis au chômage**	*[Zhuh SWEE oh sho-MAHZH]*
I love my job	**J'aime mon travail**	*[ZHEM moh(n) trah-VY]*
I work part time	**Je travaille à temps partiel**	*[Zhuh trah-VY ah tah(n) par-SYEL]*
I work as a ___	**Je travaille en tant que**	*[Zhuh trah-VY ahn TAH(n) kuh]*

English	French	Pronunciation
Waiter	**Serveur / Serveuse**	*[sair-VUHR / sair-VUHZ]*
Dentist	**Dentiste**	*[dahn-TEEST]*
Driver	**Chauffeur / Chauffeuse**	*[SHOH-fuhr / SHOH-fuhz]*
Nurse	**Infirmier / Infirmière**	*[an-FEER-mee-ay / an-FEER-mee-ehr]*
Electrician	**Électricien / Électricienne**	*[ay-lek-TREE-syan / ay-lek-TREE-syen]*

English	French	Pronunciation
Doctor	**Médecin**	[mayd-SAN]
Businessman/ woman	**Homme / Femme d'affaires**	[ohm / fam dah-FEHR]
Surgeon	**Chirurgien / Chirurgienne**	[sheer-UR-jyan / sheer-UR-jyen]
Doorman	**Concierge**	[kohn-SYAIRZH]
Secretary	**Secrétaire**	[suh-kruh-TEHR]
Soldier	**Militaire**	[mee-lee-TEHR]
Reporter	**Journaliste**	[zhoor-nah-LEEST]
Professor	**Professeur**	[proh-fay-SUHR]
Police officer	**Policier**	[poh-lee-SYAY]
Postman	**Facteur / Factrice**	[fak-TUHR / fak-TREES]
Photographer	**Photographe**	[foh-toh-GRAHF]
Pilot	**Pilote**	[pee-LOHT]
Painter	**Peintre**	[PAN-truh]
Mechanic	**Mécanicien / Mécanicienne**	[may-kah-nee-SYAN / may-kah-nee-SYEN]
Lifeguard	**Maître nageur**	[MEHT-ruh nah-ZHUHR]
Housekeeper	**Gouvernante**	[goo-vair-NAHNT]
Gardener	**Jardinier**	[zhar-dee-NYAY]
Farmer	**Agriculteur**	[ah-gree-kool-TUHR]
Flight attendant	**Hôtesse de l'air**	[oh-TESS duh LEHR]
Fireman	**Pompier**	[pohm-PYAY]
Engineer	**Ingénieur**	[an-zhay-NYUHR]
Architect	**Architecte**	[ar-shee-TEHKT]
Salesman	**Vendeur / Vendeuse**	[von-DUHR / von-DUHZ]
Veterinarian	**Vétérinaire**	[vay-tay-ree-NAIR]
Pharmacist	**Pharmacien / Pharmacienne**	[far-mah-SYAN / far-mah-SYEN]

Speak Abroad
Academy

Making plans

The best part of learning a new language and making new friends is sharing activities with them that allow you to discover a new culture. These are the main sentences you'll need when making plans in French.

English	French	Pronunciation
Let's watch a movie this week	Regardons un film cette semaine	[ruh-GAR-don uh FEELM set suh-MEN]
Let's do something fun	Faisons quelque chose d'amusant	[fuh-ZON kel-kuh SHOHZ dah-mew-ZON]
Let's go to the beach this weekend	Allons à la plage ce week-end	[ah-LON ah lah PLAHZ suh WEEK-end]
Let's play football	Jouons au football	[zhoo-ON oh FOOT-ball]
Are you free tonight?	Es-tu libre ce soir?	[ay-TEW LEE-bruh suh SWAHR?]
When are you free to hang out?	Quand es-tu libre pour sortir ?	[kon ay-TEW LEE-bruh poor sor-TEER?]
I'm only free in the evening	Je ne suis libre que le soir	[zhuh nuh SWEE LEE-bruh kuh luh SWAHR]
Can I come with you?	Puis-je venir avec toi ?	[pweezh vuh-NEER ah-VEK twah?]
What time should we meet up?	À quelle heure devons-nous nous rejoindre ?	[ah kel UHR duh-VOHN noo roo-ZHWAHN-druh?]
Where should we go?	Où devrions-nous aller ?	[oo duh-VREE-on noo ah-LAY?]
What should we do?	Que devrions-nous faire ?	[kuh duh-VREE-on noo FAIR?]
Let's go to a party	Allons à une fête	[ah-LON ah ewn FET]
Let's stay at home	Restons à la maison	[res-TON ah lah may-ZON]
Let's go out tonight	Sortons ce soir	[sor-TON suh SWAHR]
I'll meet you at the ____ at ____	Je te retrouve au ____ à ____	[zhuh tuh ruh-TROOV oh ____ ah ____]
What's your plan for today?	Quel est ton programme pour aujourd'hui ?	[kel ay ton PROH-gram poor oh-zhoor-DWEE?]
What are you doing tomorrow?	Que fais-tu demain ?	[kuh fay-TEW duh-MAN?]
Let's go to the bar	Allons au bar	[ah-LON oh BAR]
Let's eat in this restaurant	Mangeons dans ce restaurant	[mon-ZHON don suh res-toh-RON]

English	French	Pronunciation
Let's spend the night in a hotel	**Passons la nuit à l'hôtel**	[pah-SON lah NWEE ah loh-TEL]
Who's coming with you?	**Qui vient avec toi ?**	[kee vyen ah-VEK twah?]
Let's try something new	**Essayons quelque chose de nouveau**	[es-SAY-yon kel-kuh SHOHZ duh noo-VOH]
Do you want to travel with me?	**Veux-tu voyager avec moi?**	[vuh-TEW voy-ah-ZHAY ah-VEK mwah?]
Yes, let's go abroad	**Partons à l'étranger**	[par-TON ah lay-tron-ZHAY]
When do you want me to pick you up?	**Quand veux-tu que je vienne te chercher ?**	[kon vuh-TEW kuh zhuh vyen tuh sher-SHAY?]
How much time do you want to spend with me tonight?	**Combien de temps veux-tu passer avec moi ce soir?**	[kom-BYAN duh TAN vuh-TEW pah-SAY ah-VEK mwah suh SWAHR?]

Flirting

Bonjour, mes amis! French culture has long been known for its appreciation of its language, and the people of France are no exception. When it comes to engaging with foreigners, the French have a particular fondness for those who make an effort to converse in their native tongue, and the American accent is widely admired. If you're looking to win some hearts and minds while traveling in the City of Love, incorporating a few key French phrases into your repertoire might just do the trick. Take it from us: these simple sentences could help you charm your way into the heart of your French crush!

English	French	Pronunciation
You look gorgeous	**Tu es très beau / très belle**	[TU ay TRAY boh / TRAY bell]
Can I buy you a drink?	**Puis-je t'offrir un verre?**	[PWEEZH toh-FREER uhn VEHR]
Are you single?	**Es-tu célibataire?**	[ay-TU say-lee-bah-TAIR]
I'm single	**Je suis célibataire**	[zhuh SWEE say-lee-bah-TAIR]
Can I join you?	**Puis-je me joindre à toi?**	[PWEEZH muh ZHWANDR ah TWA]
This dress looks amazing on you	**Cette robe te va à merveille**	[SET rob tuh VAH ah mehr-VAY]
You have beautiful eyes	**Tu as de beaux yeux**	[TU ah duh BOH ZYUH]
Can I have your number?	**Puis-je avoir ton numéro ?**	[PWEEZH ah-VWAR ton nyoo-MAY-roh]

Speak Abroad
Academy

English	French	Pronunciation
Your smile is contagious	**Ton sourire est contagieux**	*[TON soo-REER ay kon-tah-ZHYUH]*
Your hair is beautiful	**Tes cheveux sont magnifiques**	*[TAY shuh-VUH sohn mah-nee-FEEK]*
Can I add you on ___?	**Puis-je t'ajouter sur ___?**	*[PWEEZH tah-zhoo-TAY suhr ___]*
Are you seeing anyone?	**Tu sors avec quelqu'un ?**	*[TU sor ah-VEK kel-KUN]*
I'm falling for you	**Je suis en train de tomber amoureux de toi**	*[zhuh SWEE on TRAHN duh tom-BAY ah-moo-ruh-ZUH duh TWA]*
How are you still single?	**Comment se fait-il que tu sois toujours célibataire ?**	*[koh-MAHN suh fay-TEEL kuh TU swah too-ZHOOR say-lee-bah-TAIR]*
Can we get together sometime?	**On peut se voir un jour ?**	*[on PUH suh VWAHR uhn ZHOOR]*
I'd like to spend more time with you	**J'aimerais passer plus de temps avec toi**	*[ZHEM-ray pah-SAY ploo duh TAHN ah-VEK TWA]*
You look amazing	**Tu es superbe**	*[TU ay soo-PERB]*
I can't get enough of you	**Je n'en ai jamais assez de toi**	*[zhuh non ay ZHAH-may ah-SAY duh TWA]*
Would you like to go on a date with me?	**Aimerais-tu sortir avec moi ?**	*[em-RAY TU sor-TEER ah-VEK MWA]*
Would you like to have dinner with me?	**Aimerais-tu dîner avec moi ?**	*[em-RAY TU dee-NAY ah-VEK MWA]*
I'd like to see you again	**J'aimerais te revoir**	*[ZHEM-ray tuh ruh-VWAHR]*
I love this about you	**J'aime ça chez toi**	*[ZHEM sah SHAY TWA]*

Common slang

The French language, like many languages, has many common slang words that you'll hear daily if you're in a French-speaking country. These words are usually short and easy to use, so you'll be able to quickly master them. Here are some of the most common slang words:

English	French	Pronunciation
To eat	**Bouffer**	*[BOO-fay]*
To flirt	**Draguer**	*[DRAH-gay]*
A thing	**Un truc**	*[uhN TROOK]*

English	French	Pronunciation
A guy	**Un type, un mec**	*[uhN TEEP, uhN MEK]*
A woman	**Une meuf**	*[oon MUHF]*
That sucks	**C'est nul**	*[say NYOOL]*
Perfect	**Nickel !**	*[nee-KEL]*
That's great	**C'est top**	*[say TOP]*
10 euros	**10 balles**	*[DEES BAL]*
Cigarette	**Une clope**	*[oon KLOP]*
To like something	**Kiffer**	*[KEE-fay]*
Friend	**Pote**	*[POHT]*
Ugly	**Moche**	*[MOSH]*

Here's a little bonus for you. Have you ever heard of 'Verlan' ? It's a particular characteristic of French argot featuring inversion of syllables in a word. It is quite popular among the youth and you're likely to hear some of these words in France.

For example:

Verlan	Pronunciation	French Meaning	English Meaning
cimer	*[SEE mehr]*	**merci**	thank you
ouf	*[OOF]*	**fou**	crazy
vénère	*[VAY nair]*	**énervé**	angry
relou	*[ruh LOO]*	**lourd**	annoying
zarbi	*[zahr BEE]*	**bizarre**	weird

Building connections

CHAPTER 18

SHOPPING & DINING OUT

France and especially Paris is famous for its luxury shops and many markets, that's why shopping is a must-do in France. Moreover, the French culture has a very strict dining etiquette and the French service in restaurants is famous for its quality. For example, dinner is usually served after 7pm, you don't switch the knife and fork back and forth, fork and knife at 4 and 8pm means that you are still eating and if they are placed diagonally together it means that you are done.

Throughout this chapter we'll help you with the common phrases and words you should know to have a good time shopping and dining out in a French-speaking country.

Practicalities

It's time to embark on a culinary escapade through the streets of France! Imagine savoring a flaky croissant for breakfast, indulging in a coq au vin masterpiece for dinner, or relishing the delicate flavors of a *tarte tatin*. French food isn't just a meal; it's a symphony of taste, from escargot to crème brûlée and you should definitely try it if you have the opportunity to do it!

The following table represents the words you must know to be able to get a seat and order in a French restaurant:

English	French	Pronunciation
Can I book a table for ___ people?	Puis-je réserver une table pour ___ personnes ?	[PWEEZH reh-zay-VAYR oon TABL poor ___ pair-SON]
How long is the wait for a table?	Quel est le temps d'attente pour avoir une table ?	[KEHL ay luh TAHN dah-TONT poor ah-VWAHR oon TABL]
Can I reserve a table for tonight?	Puis-je réserver une table pour ce soir ?	[PWEEZH reh-zay-VAYR oon TABL poor suh SWAHR]
A table for two please	Une table pour deux s'il vous plaît	[OON TABL poor DUH seel voo PLAY]
I have a reservation	J'ai une réservation	[ZHEY oon reh-zayr-vah-SYON]
Is this restaurant accessible to wheelchairs?	Est-ce que ce restaurant est accessible aux fauteuils roulants ?	[ES kuh suh res-toh-RAHN eh ahk-SEH-see-bluh oh foh-TUH roo-LAHN]

English	French	Pronunciation
Are children allowed in this restaurant?	**Les enfants sont-ils admis dans ce restaurant ?**	*[LAYZ ahn-FAHN sohn TEELZ ahd-MEE dahn suh res-toh-RAHN]*
Do you serve alcohol?	**Est-ce que vous servez de l'alcool ?**	*[ES kuh voo SER-vay duh lahl-KOHL]*
Can I have my steak cooked rare / medium rare/ medium/ well done?	**Puis-je avoir mon steak bleu, saignant, à point, bien cuit**	*[PWEEZH ah-VWAHR mohn STEK bluh, sahn-YAHN, ah PWAHN, BYAN kwee]*
Takeaway	**À emporter**	*[AH ahn-por-TAY]*
Can I please order?	**Puis-je commander ?**	*[PWEEZH koh-mahn-DAY]*
Gluten-free	**Sans gluten**	*[SAHN GLOO-ten]*
Dairy-free	**Sans produits laitiers**	*[SAHN proh-DWEE lay-TYAY]*
Vegan	**Vegan**	*[VAY-gahn]*
Vegetarian	**Végétarien**	*[vay-zhay-tah-RYAN]*
I don't eat meat	**Je ne mange pas de viande**	*[zhuh nuh MAHNZH pah duh VYAHND]*
I think this is the wrong order	**Je pense que ce n'est pas la bonne commande**	*[zhuh PAHNSS kuh suh neh pah lah BUN koh-MAHND]*
Can I get the bill please?	**Puis-je avoir l'addition s'il vous plaît ?**	*[PWEEZH ah-VWAHR lah-dee-SYON seel voo PLAY]*
What would you recommend?	**Que me recommandez-vous ?**	*[kuh muh ruh-koh-mahn-DAY voo]*
What's today's special?	**Quel est le plat du jour ?**	*[KEHL ay luh PLAH doo ZHOOR]*

Food & drink

France is internationally recognised for its gastronomy to the point that the French gastronomic meal has been recognized as a UNESCO cultural heritage. Throughout this section we will introduce you to famous French food as well as common meals in French.

English	French	Pronunciation
Onion soup	**la soupe à l'oignon**	*[lah SOOP ah l'AW-nyohn]*
Duck confit	**le confit de canard**	*[luh kohn-FEE duh kah-NAR]*
Beef tartare	**le steak tartare**	*[luh STEK tar-TAR]*
Mussels	**les moules (f)**	*[lay MOOL]*
Snails	**les escargots (m)**	*[lay es-kar-GO]*

Speak Abroad
Academy

English	French	Pronunciation
Pasta	**Les pâtes (f)**	*[lay PAHT]*
Rice	**Le riz**	*[luh REE]*
Red/white wine	**Le vin rouge/blanc**	*[luh VAN ROOZH/blahn]*
Water	**L'eau (f)**	*[loh]*
Soda	**La boisson gazeuse**	*[lah bwah-SOHN gah-ZUHZ]*
Beer	**La bière**	*[lah BYEHR]*
French fries	**Les frites (f)**	*[lay FREET]*
Cheese	**Le fromage**	*[luh froh-MAHZH]*
Fried egg	**L'Œuf au plat (m)**	*[luhf oh PLAH]*
Fish	**Le poisson**	*[luh pwah-SOHN]*
Roast chicken	**Le poulet rôti**	*[luh POO-lay roh-TEE]*
Yogurt	**Le yaourt**	*[luh yah-OORT]*
Ice cream	**La glace**	*[lah GLAHS]*
Seafood	**Les fruits de mer (m)**	*[lay FRWEE duh mehr]*
Porridge	**Le porridge**	*[luh po-REEJ]*
Ham	**Le jambon**	*[luh zhahm-BOHN]*
Shrimp	**La crevette**	*[lah kruh-VET]*
Juice	**Le jus**	*[luh ZHOO]*
Grilled	**Grillé**	*[gree-YAY]*
Smoked	**Fumé**	*[foo-MAY]*
Chocolate cake	**Le gâteau au chocolat**	*[luh gah-TOH oh shoh-koh-LAH]*
Starter	**L'entrée (f)**	*[LON-tray]*
Main course	**Le plat principal**	*[luh PLAH pran-see-PAL]*
Appetizer	**L'amuse-bouche (m)**	*[lah-MYOOZ boosh]*
Dessert	**Le dessert**	*[luh deh-SAIR]*
Liquor / Alcohol	**L'alcool (m)**	*[lal-KOL]*
Beverages	**Les boissons (f)**	*[lay bwa-SON]*
Salads	**Les salades (f)**	*[lay sah-LAHD]*
Sides	**Les accompagnements (m)**	*[lay ah-kohm-pah-NYUH-mahn]*

Dining out phrases

In the continuity of this chapter, we're providing you with the phrases you might need if you're dining out in a French-speaking country, which is definitely a must-do in France.

English	French	Pronunciation
This is delicious	C'est délicieux	[SAY day-lee-SYUH]
I want to try the local specialties	Je veux essayer les spécialités locales	[zhuh VUH eh-say-YAY lay spay-see-ah-lee-TAY loh-KAHL]
I'd like another glass of ___	J'aimerais un autre verre de ___	[zhaym-RAY uh NOH-truh VEHR duh ___]
Are you enjoying your food?	Est-ce que le repas vous plaît ?	[ess kuh luh ruh-PAH voo PLAY]
What will you order?	Qu'allez-vous commander ?	[kah-LAY voo koh-mahn-DAY]
Your food looks so delicious	Vos plats ont l'air délicieux	[voh PLAH ohn LEHR day-lee-SYUH]
Can I try some?	Je peux goûter ?	[zhuh PUH goo-TAY]
Will you share with me?	Veux-tu partager avec moi ?	[vuh TU par-tah-ZHAY ah-VEK mwah]
Do you want a dessert?	Voulez-vous un dessert ?	[voo-LAY voo uh deh-SEHR]
Is this fresh?	Est-ce que c'est frais ?	[ess kuh SAY fray]
This will be my last glass	C'est mon dernier verre	[SAY mohn dern-YAY VEHR]
My compliments to the chef	Mes compliments au chef	[may KOM-plee-mahn oh shehf]
Do you want to share this dish?	Voulez-vous partager ce plat ?	[voo-LAY voo par-tah-ZHAY suh PLAH]
I will have the ___	Je vais prendre le ___	[zhuh vay PRAHN-druh luh ___]
Can I change my order?	Est-ce que je peux changer ma commande ?	[ess kuh zhuh PUH shahn-ZHAY mah koh-MAHND]
You deserve a tip	Vous méritez un pourboire	[voo may-ree-TAY uhn poor-BWAHR]
The waiter will take you to your table	Le serveur va vous conduire à votre table	[luh sair-VUHR vah voo kohn-DWEER ah voh-truh TAH-bluh]

Shopping words

Be it strolling through a vibrant marché or stepping into the opulence of Parisian boutiques, mastering the following words is your key to navigating the treasures of a French-speaking land with flair!

Groceries

English	French	Pronunciation
The groceries	**Les courses**	*[lay KOORSS]*
Fruit	**Un fruit**	*[uhn FWEE]*
Vegetable	**Un légume**	*[uhn lay-GOOM]*
Apple	**La pomme**	*[lah PUHM]*
Carrot	**La carotte**	*[lah kah-ROHT]*
Grape	**Le raisin**	*[luh ray-ZAN]*
Peach	**La pêche**	*[lah PESH]*
Strawberry	**La fraise**	*[lah FREHZ]*
Pineapple	**L'ananas (m)**	*[lah-nah-NAH]*
Watermelon	**La pastèque**	*[lah pah-STEK]*
Tomato	**La tomate**	*[lah toh-MAHT]*
Eggplant	**L'aubergine (f)**	*[loh-bair-ZHEEN]*
Cucumber	**Le concombre**	*[luh kon-KOM-bruh]*
Lettuce	**La laitue**	*[lah lay-TYOO]*
Potato	**La pomme de terre**	*[lah PUHM duh TAIR]*
Pepper	**Le poivre**	*[luh PWAHV]*
Salt	**Le sel**	*[luh SEL]*
Cooking oil	**L'huile de cuisson (f)**	*[l'weel duh kwee-SON]*

Toiletries

English	French	Pronunciation
Shampoo	**Le shampooing**	*[luh SHAHN-pwan]*
Conditioner	**L'après-shampooing (m)**	*[la-PRAY SHAHN-pwan]*
Hair Brush	**La brosse à cheveux**	*[lah BROHS ah shuh-VUH]*
Toothbrush	**La brosse à dents**	*[lah BROHS ah DAHN]*
Toothpaste	**Le dentifrice**	*[luh DAHN-tee-freess]*
Sunscreen	**La crème solaire**	*[lah KREM so-LAIR]*

English	French	Pronunciation
Soap	**Le savon**	*[luh sah-VOHN]*
Razor	**Le rasoir**	*[luh rah-SWAHR]*
Make up	**Le maquillage**	*[luh mah-kee-YAHJ]*

Clothing Items

English	French	Pronunciation
Clothing Items	**Les vêtements**	*[lay VET-mahn]*
Suit	**Un costume**	*[uhn kos-TEWM]*
Blouse	**Un chemisier**	*[uhn shuh-MEE-syay]*
T-Shirt	**Un t-shirt**	*[uhn tee-SHIRT]*
Pants	**Un pantalon (m) - singular**	*[uhn PAHN-ta-lohn]*
Jacket	**Une veste**	*[ewn VEST]*
Sweater	**Un pull**	*[uhn PEWL]*
Coat	**Un manteau**	*[uhn mahn-TOH]*
Sock	**Une chaussette**	*[ewn shoh-SET]*
Shoe	**Une chaussure**	*[ewn shoh-SURE]*
Tracksuit	**Un survêtement**	*[uhn sur-VET-mahn]*
Sweatshirt	**Un sweat-shirt**	*[uhn SWEAT-shirt]*
Dress	**Une robe**	*[ewn ROB]*
Skirt	**Une jupe**	*[ewn ZHOOP]*
Cap	**Une casquette**	*[ewn kas-KET]*

Tech Essentials

English	French	Pronunciation
Phone Charger	**Un chargeur de téléphone**	*[uhn SHAR-jur duh tay-lay-FON]*
Power Bank	**Une batterie externe**	*[oon baht-REE ex-TERN]*
Laptop	**Un ordinateur portable**	*[uhn or-dee-na-TUR por-TAH-bluh]*
Headphones	**Un casque**	*[uhn KASK]*
Usb Flash Drive	**Une clé USB**	*[oon klay oo-ESS-bay]*
Universal Adapter	**Un adaptateur universel**	*[uhn ah-dap-tah-TUR oo-nee-ver-SEL]*

English	French	Pronunciation
Keyboard	**Un clavier**	*[uhn kla-VYAY]*
Mouse	**Une souris**	*[oon soo-REE]*
Bluetooth speaker	**Une enceinte bluetooth**	*[oon on-SENT bloo-TOOTH]*
Screen	**Un écran**	*[uhn ay-KRAHN]*

Shopping phrases

So, now that we're done with the important shopping words, it's time to reveal the essential shopping phrases to have in your shopping arsenal when exploring a French-speaking destination.

It's no secret that we all love to shop. It's a way to immortalize those fond memories by taking home something that serves as a sweet reminder of a time well spent. Whether it is a French scarf that caught your eye or a pretty painting by a local artist, these are the essential phrases you'll need to communicate your needs clearly:

English	French	Pronunciation
I would like to try this	**J'aimerais essayer ça**	*[ZHEM-ray eh-say-YAY sah]*
I'm looking for ____	**Je cherche ____**	*[zhuh SHERSH]*
Could you tell me where I can find ____?	**Pourriez-vous me dire où je peux trouver ____? (formal)**	*[poor-YAY voo muh DEER oo zhuh puh troo-VAY]*
Where is the women/men's section?	**Où se trouve la section femmes/hommes ?**	*[oo suh TROOV lah sek-SYON fahm / ohm]*
Could you help me?	**Pourriez-vous m'aider ? (formal)**	*[poor-YAY voo may-DAY]*
Can I have a different size?	**Puis-je avoir une autre taille ?**	*[pwee zhuh ah-VWAR oon oh-truh TAI]*
I would like this in a size ____?	**Je voudrais ça en taille ____**	*[zhuh voo-DRAY sah on TAI]*
Where are the fitting rooms?	**Où se trouvent les cabines d'essayage ?**	*[oo suh TROOV lay kah-BEEN deh-say-YAJ]*
What time do you close?	**À quelle heure fermez-vous ?**	*[ah kel UHR fer-MAY voo]*
Can I return this?	**Puis-je retourner ça ?**	*[pwee zhuh ruh-toor-NAY sah]*
Do you have this in a different color?	**Avez-vous ce vêtement dans une autre couleur ?**	*[ah-VAY voo suh vet-MON don oon oh-truh koo-LUHR]*

English	French	Pronunciation
On what floor can I find the ___?	A quel étage puis-je trouver le ___?	[ah kel ay-TAHZH pwee zhuh troo-VAY luh]
Does this suit me?	Est-ce que ça me va ?	[ess kuh sah muh VAH]
What are the available sizes for this?	Quelles sont les tailles disponibles pour ça ?	[kel sohn lay TAI dee-spon-EE-bluh poor sah]
This is too expensive.	C'est trop cher	[say troh SHER]
It's the discount season.	C'est la saison des soldes	[say lah say-ZON day SOLD]

Paying for something

When traveling abroad, you're expected to buy a lot of things. These are the essential sentences you'll need in that case or whether you're simply in a French-speaking country and need to buy something.

English	French	Pronunciation
Do you have discounts?	Avez-vous des remises ?	[AH-vay voo day re-MEES?]
I am going to buy this.	Je vais acheter ça	[zhuh vay ah-SHUH-tay sah]
How much does this cost?	Combien ça coûte ?	[kohm-BYAN sah KOOT?]
Do you take credit cards?	Acceptez-vous les cartes de crédit ?	[ahk-SEP-tay voo lay KART duh KRAY-dee?]
Cash only	En espèces seulement	[ahn es-PEHS suhl-MOHN]
Is this the final price?	Est-ce le prix final ?	[ehs luh PREE fee-NAL?]
Do you accept checks?	Acceptez-vous les chèques ?	[ahk-SEP-tay voo lay shek?]
I would like to pay ___ by cash and ___ by credit card	Je souhaite payer ___ en espèces et ___ par carte de crédit	[zhuh soo-ET pay-YAY ___ ahn es-PEHS ay ___ par KART duh KRAY-dee]
What are the paying methods available?	Quels sont les modes de paiement disponibles ?	[kel sohn lay mod duh pay-MAHN dee-spon-EE-bluh?]
Does your store accept contactless payments?	Votre magasin accepte-t-il les paiements sans contact ?	[voh-truh mah-gah-ZAN ahk-SEP-tuh teel lay pay-MAHN sahn kon-TAKT?]
I want a refund.	Je veux un remboursement	[zhuh vuh uh(n) rahm-BOOR-suh-mahn]
I want a receipt for this.	Je veux un reçu	[zhuh vuh uh(n) ruh-SU]

CHAPTER 19

TRAVEL & TRANSPORTATION

Embark on a language journey for countless adventures! Whether you're dreaming of ordering a divine croissant at a Parisian boulangerie or navigating the bustling markets in Provence, learning French opens doors to extraordinary experiences. Picture strolling through the Louvre armed with your newfound language skills or effortlessly conversing with locals in the charming streets of Bordeaux. This chapter is your gateway to mastering the essentials and unlocking a world of French wonders!

Getting around

The main part of traveling and visiting a new country is getting around. You'll need to know what to say to take the bus or the subway. You'll probably have to ask for directions and you'll need to know the names of some of the most frequented places. That's what we'll provide you with throughout this section:

English	French	Pronunciation
How do I get to the train station?	Comment je vais à la gare ?	[koh-MAHN zhuh vay ah lah GAR]
What time is the next train to ___?	À quelle heure est le prochain train pour ___?	[ah KELL eur eh luh proh-SHAN tran poor ___]
Where is the bus stop?	Où se trouve l'arrêt de bus?	[oo suh TROOV lah-RAY duh BEWSS]
Where can I buy tickets for the ___?	Où puis-je acheter des billets pour le ___?	[oo pwee zhuh ah-SHAY day bee-YEH poor luh ___]
Where can I get a taxi?	Où puis-je trouver un taxi ?	[oo pwee zhuh TROO-vay uhn TAX-ee]
Is this the right way to ___?	Est-ce le bon chemin pour aller au ___?	[ess luh BON shuh-MAN poor ah-LAY oh ___]
Where is the nearest ___?	Où se trouve le ___ le plus proche ?	[oo suh TROOV luh ___ luh plew PROSH]
It's next to the ___	C'est à côté du ___ (de la)	[say ah koh-TAY dew ___ (duh lah)]
It's to the left, right	C'est à gauche, à droite	[say ah GOHSH, ah DWAHT]
Where is the subway station?	Où se trouve la station de métro ?	[oo suh TROOV lah stah-SYON duh MAY-troh]

English	French	Pronunciation
Does this subway go to ___?	Ce métro va-t-il à ___?	[suh MAY-troh vah-TEEL ah ___]
Can you take me to ___?	Pouvez-vous m'emmener à ___?	[poo-vay VOO mahn-MAY-nay ah ___]
Can you drop me here please?	Pouvez-vous me déposer ici s'il vous plaît ?	[poo-vay VOO muh day-poh-ZAY ee-SEE seel voo pleh]
How do I get there by foot?	Comment s'y rendre à pied ?	[koh-MAHN see rahnd ah pyay]
Can I rent a car?	Puis-je louer une voiture ?	[pwee-zhuh loo-AY uhn vwah-TEWR]

English	French	Pronunciation
The beach	La plage	[la PLAHZH]
The airport	L'aéroport (m)	[lay-er-OH-por]
The shopping center	Le centre commercial	[luh SAHN-truh koh-mayr-SYAL]
The park	Le parc	[luh PARK]
The museum	Le musée	[luh MYU-zay]
The bakery	La boulangerie	[la boo-lawn-ZHUH-ree]
The hospital	L'hôpital (m)	[loh-pee-TAL]
The library	La bibliothèque	[la bee-blee-oh-TEHK]
The bank	La banque	[la BAHNK]
The market	Le marché	[luh mar-SHAY]
The gift shop	La boutique de souvenirs	[la boo-TEEK duh soo-vuh-NEER]
The barbershop	Le salon de coiffure	[luh sah-LAWN duh kwah-FUR]
Pharmacy	La pharmacie	[la far-mah-SEE]

Signs & notices

Signs and notices are a main part of any country's streets. French-speaking countries don't represent an exception and that's why you need to know the following signs and notices when traveling there.

English	French	Pronunciation
Out of order	Hors service	[OR sair-VEES]
Entrance	L'entrée (f)	[LON-tray]
Exit	La sortie	[la sor-TEE]

English	French	Pronunciation
Emergency exit	**La sortie de secours**	*[la sor-TEE duh suh-KOOR]*
Toilets	**Les toilettes (f)**	*[lay twah-LET]*
Ticket	**Un billet**	*[uhn bee-YAY]*
Information	**Une information**	*[ewn an-for-mah-SYON]*
No smoking	**Interdit de fumer**	*[an-tair-DEE duh fyoo-MAY]*
Disabled	**Handicapé**	*[an-dee-ka-PAY]*
Drinking water	**L'eau potable (f)**	*[loh poh-TAB]*
Warning	**Un avertissement**	*[uhn ah-vair-tees-MON]*
Security	**La sécurité**	*[la say-kew-ree-TAY]*
No entry	**Entrée interdite**	*[on-TRAY an-tair-DEET]*
Keep off the grass	**Défense de marcher sur l'herbe**	*[day-FONS duh mar-SHAY sur lairb]*
Be careful	**Attention**	*[ah-ton-SYON]*
Pedestrians only	**Piétons seulement**	*[pyeh-TON seul-MON]*
Children crossing	**Enfants traversant la rue**	*[on-FON tra-vair-SAN la roo]*
Fire extinguisher	**Un extincteur**	*[uhn ex-ting-TAIR]*
No mobile phone	**Pas de téléphone portable**	*[pah duh tay-lay-FON por-TAH-bluh]*
No camera	**Pas d'appareil photo**	*[pah dah-par-AY foh-TOH]*
Wear a mask	**Porter un masque**	*[por-TAY uhn MASK]*
Slippery road	**Route glissante**	*[root glee-SANT]*
Do not disturb	**Ne pas déranger**	*[nuh pah day-RAHN-zhay]*

At the airport

The airport is an essential part of traveling and it's always helpful to speak the local language there. We're going to provide you with the main phrases and words you'll need when you are in a French-speaking airport.

English	French	Pronunciation
Checked baggage	**Un bagage enregistré**	*[uhn ba-GAZH ahn-reh-JIS-tray]*
Hand luggage	**Un bagage à main**	*[uhn ba-GAZH ah MAHN]*
Delayed	**En retard**	*[ahn ruh-TAR]*
Customs	**La Douane**	*[lah DWAN]*

English	French	Pronunciation
What is the departure gate for the flight to ___?	Quelle est la porte d'embarquement pour le vol vers ___?	[KEHL eh lah PORT dahm-bar-keh-MAHN poor luh vol VEHR ___?]
What is the purpose of your trip?	Quel est le but de votre voyage ?	[KEHL eh luh BYOOT duh voh-truh vwa-YAHZH?]
Please do not leave any bags unattended	Veuillez ne pas laisser de sacs sans surveillance	[VUH-yay nuh PAH lay-SAY duh SAK sahn suur-VAY-yahnss]
Flight ___ is now boarding	L'embarquement du vol ___ est en cours	[lahm-bar-keh-MAHN doo vol ___ eh ahn KOOR]
Flight ___ has been canceled	Le vol ___ a été annulé	[luh vol ___ ah eh-TAY ahn-nyoo-LAY]
Flight ___ has been delayed	Le vol ___ a été retardé	[luh vol ___ ah eh-TAY ruh-TAR-day]
Would passengers ___ please come to ___ ?	Le passager ___ est prié de se rendre à ___	[luh pah-sah-JAY ___ eh pree-AY duh suh rahn-druh ah ___]
Please make your way to gate ___	Veuillez vous rendre à la porte ___	[VUH-yay voo rahn-druh ah lah PORT ___]
Do you have any bags to check?	Avez-vous des bagages à enregistrer ?	[ah-VAY voo day ba-GAZH ahn-reh-JIS-tray?]
May I have your passport please?	Puis-je avoir votre passeport ?	[pwee zhah-VWAR voh-truh pass-POR?]
Would you like a window seat?	Voulez-vous un siège à côté du hublot ?	[voo-LAY voo uhn SYEHZH ah koh-TAY doo oo-BLOH?]
Here's your boarding pass	Voici votre carte d'embarquement	[vwah-SEE voh-truh kart dahm-bar-keh-MAHN]
Your flight leaves from gate ___	Votre vol part de la porte ___	[voh-truh vol PAR duh lah PORT ___]
Please proceed to security	Veuillez passer à la sécurité	[VUH-yay pah-SAY ah lah say-koo-ree-TAY]
Where is the baggage claim?	Où se trouve la récupération des bagages ?	[oo suh TROOV lah ray-kew-pay-rah-SYOHN day ba-GAZH?]
Could you tell me where the customs are?	Pourriez-vous me dire où se trouve la douane ?	[poor-YAY voo muh DEER oo suh TROOV lah DWAN?]
Could you tell me where Terminal ___ is?	Pourriez-vous me dire où se trouve le terminal ___?	[poor-YAY voo muh DEER oo suh TROOV luh ter-mee-NAHL ___?]

Hotel & accommodation

If you're visiting a French-speaking country, you'll need a place to stay, probably a hotel. Throughout this part we will present the basic phrases and words to help you with your accommodation in French.

English	French	Pronunciation
I have a reservation	J'ai une réservation	[ZHEH oon ray-zair-va-SYOHN]
I booked a room online. It's under ___	J'ai réservé une chambre en ligne. C'est au nom de ___	[ZHEH ray-zair-VAY oon SHAHM-bruh ahn LEEN-yuh]-[SEH toh NOHN duh ___]
Do you have any vacancies?	Avez-vous des chambres libres ?	[AH-vay VOO day SHAHM-bruhs LEE-bruh]
I'd like a single/ double/ triple/ twin room/ suite, please	Je voudrais une chambre simple/ double/ triple/ jumelle / une suite, s'il vous plaît.	[Zhuh voo-DRAY oon SHAHM-bruh SAM-pluh/ DOOB-luh/ TREE-pluh/ zhoo-MELL/ oon SWEET, seel voo PLEH]
Where are the elevators?	Où se trouvent les ascenseurs ?	[OO suh TROOV lay ah-sahn-SUHR]
What time is checkout?	À quelle heure est le check out?	[Ah kel UHR ay luh CHECK OUT]
Could you fill out this registration form?	Pourriez-vous remplir ce formulaire d'inscription ?	[Poor-YAY VOO rahm-PLEER suh for-myoo-LAHR dahn-skreep-SYOHN]
I'm sorry, we don't have any vacancies.	Je suis désolé, nous n'avons pas de chambres libres.	[Zhuh SWEE day-zoh-LAY noo nah-VOHN pah duh SHAHM-bruhs LEE-bruh]
I'm sorry, we're completely booked.	Je suis désolé, nous sommes complets.	[Zhuh SWEE day-zoh-LAY noo SUHM kohm-PLAY]
I'd like to check out.	Je voudrais faire le check out. / Je voudrais régler la chambre.	[Zhuh voo-DRAY FAIR luh CHECK OUT / Zhuh voo-DRAY ray-GLAY lah SHAHM-bruh]
How was your stay?	Comment s'est passé votre séjour ?	[Koh-MAHN seh pah-SAY VOH-truh say-ZHOOR]
Could I have the room key, please?	Puis-je avoir la clé de la chambre, s'il vous plaît ?	[PWEEzh ah-VWAHR lah KLAY duh lah SHAHM-bruh, seel voo PLEH]
Can I see the room, please?	Puis-je voir la chambre, s'il vous plaît ?	[PWEEzh vwah lah SHAHM-bruh, seel voo PLEH]

English	French	Pronunciation
What time is breakfast?	À quelle heure est le petit-déjeuner?	[Ah kel UHR ay luh puh-TEE day-zhuh-NAY]
Where is the restaurant?	Où se trouve le restaurant ?	[OO suh TROOV luh res-toh-RAHN]
Do you have any room available for ___?	Avez-vous une chambre disponible pour ___?	[AH-vay VOO oon SHAHM-bruh dee-spoh-NEEB poor ___]
Does the room have air-conditioning?	La chambre est-elle climatisée ?	[Lah SHAHM-bruh eh-TELL klee-mah-tee-ZAY]
Can someone help me with my bags?	Quelqu'un peut-il m'aider à porter mes bagages ?	[Kel-KAN puh-TEEL meh-DAY ah por-TAY may bah-GAHZH]
I'd like to book a room, please	Je voudrais réserver une chambre, s'il vous plaît	[Zhuh voo-DRAY ray-zair-VAY oon SHAHM-bruh, seel voo PLEH]
I want to call room service	Je veux appeler le service d'étage	[Zhuh VUH zah-PLAY luh sair-VEESS day-TAHZH]

English	French	Pronunciation
Motel	Un motel	[uhn moh-TELL]
Hostel	Une auberge de jeunesse	[ewn oh-BEHRZH duh zhuh-NESS]
Hotel	Un hôtel	[uhn oh-TELL]
A vacation rental	Une location de vacances	[ewn loh-ka-SYOHN duh va-KAHNS]
A single room	Une chambre simple	[ewn SHAHM-bruh sampl]
A double room	Une chambre double	[ewn SHAHM-bruh DOO-bluh]
The pool	La piscine	[lah pee-SEEN]
A shuttle service	Un service de navette	[uhn sair-VEES duh nah-VET]
The reception	La réception	[lah ray-sep-SYOHN]
The porter	Le bagagiste	[luh bah-gah-ZHEEST]
The lobby	Le hall d'entrée	[luh ohl DAHN-tray]

CHAPTER 20

HEALTH NEEDS & EMERGENCIES

Travelling is fun, going to a French-speaking country will probably be a life-changing experience. Nevertheless, we're never safe from a health problem or an emergency. In those cases, speaking the local language solves a lot of problems. That's why we are going to provide you with the main phrases and words you need to know if you're facing an emergency in a French speaking country, while hoping you won't need to use it.

General phrases

With this book, we aim to help every traveler in a French-speaking country. With that in mind, we're trying to help you with your general needs. Throughout this section, you'll learn the phrases you need to know to let someone know if you need special assistance or what your needs are.

English	French	Pronunciation
I need a wheelchair	J'ai besoin d'un fauteuil roulant	[ZHAY buh-ZWAN dun FOH-toy roo-LAN]
I need to go to the pharmacy / doctor	J'ai besoin d'aller à la pharmacie / chez le médecin	[ZHAY buh-ZWAN da-LAY ah la far-mah-SEE / shay luh may-DZAN]
I'm pregnant	Je suis enceinte	[zhuh SWEE on-SANT]
Is this safe for pregnancy?	Est-ce que ce n'est pas dangereux pour la grossesse ?	[ESS kuh suh NAY pah dan-zhuh-RUH poor la groh-SES]
I need help	J'ai besoin d'aide	[ZHAY buh-ZWAN ED]
Is there access by wheelchair?	Y a-t-il un accès en fauteuil roulant ?	[YA teel un ack-SAY on FOH-toy roo-LAN]
That's my assistance dog	C'est mon chien d'assistance	[SAY mon SHYEN dah-see-STANSS]
Is this available for people with special needs?	Y a-t-il un accès pour les personnes ayant des besoins particuliers ?	[YA teel un ack-SAY poor lay pair-SON ay-YAN day buh-ZWAN par-tick-yoo-LYAY]
Where's the nearest hospital?	Où se trouve l'hôpital le plus proche ?	[OO suh troov loh-pee-TAL luh plew PROHSH]

English	French	Pronunciation
I am looking for department ___	Je cherche le service de ___	[zhuh SHER-sh luh sair-VEESS duh ___]
I am diabetic	Je suis diabétique	[zhuh SWEE dee-ah-BAY-teek]

Health problems

Health problems usually come unexpectedly. We surely hope you enjoy your trip to the maximum and you won't need to use this part, but you need to be prepared. Throughout this section we will provide you with the phrases and words you need to express your health problems.

English	French	Pronunciation
I don't feel well	Je ne me sens pas bien	[zhuh nuh muh SAHN pah byahn]
I have a headache	J'ai mal à la tête	[zhay MAHL ah lah TEHT]
I'm going to vomit	J'ai envie de vomir	[zhay ahn-VEE duh voh-MEER]
I feel like I might faint	J'ai l'impression que je vais m'évanouir	[zhay lahm-preh-SYOHN kuh zhuh vay may-vah-NWEER]
Do you feel nauseous?	Avez-vous la nausée ?	[ah-VAY voo lah noh-ZAY]
My ___ hurts	J'ai mal au ___ (à la)	[zhay MAHL oh ___ (ah lah)]
I'm struggling to breathe	J'ai du mal à respirer	[zhay dew MAHL ah reh-spee-RAY]
I think I'm having a heart attack	Je pense que je fais une crise cardiaque	[zhuh PAHNS kuh zhuh fay ewn kreez KAR-dee-ahk]
I feel dizzy	J'ai des vertiges	[zhay day vehr-TEEZH]
I have had a seizure	J'ai eu des convulsion	[zhay ew day kohn-vool-SYOHN]
I'm having trouble to keep my eyes open	J'ai du mal à garder les yeux ouverts	[zhay dew MAHL ah gahr-DAY lay zyuh oo-VEHR]
My hands are shaking	Mes mains tremblent	[may MAN TRAM-bluh]
I am vomiting blood	Je vomis du sang	[zhuh voh-MEE dew SAHN]

English	French	Pronunciation
Headache	Un mal de tête	[uhn MAHL duh TEHT]
Stomach ache	Un mal de ventre	[uhn MAHL duh VAHN-truh]
Chest pain	Une douleur à la poitrine	[ewn doo-LUHR ah lah pwa-TREEN]

English	French	Pronunciation
Heart attack	**Une crise cardiaque**	*[ewn KREEZ kar-DYAK]*
Allergy	**Une allergie**	*[ewn ah-lair-ZHEE]*
Dizziness	**Un étourdissement**	*[uhn ay-TOOR-dees-mahn]*
Fever	**Une fièvre**	*[ewn FYEHV-ruh]*
The flu	**La grippe**	*[lah GREEP]*
Insomnia	**Une insomnie**	*[ewn an-som-NEE]*
Rash	**Une éruption cutanée**	*[ewn ay-roop-SYON koo-tah-NAY]*
Runny nose	**Le nez qui coule**	*[luh NAY kee KOOL]*
Sunburn	**Un coup de soleil**	*[uhn KOO duh soh-LAY]*
Sore throat	**Un mal de gorge**	*[uhn MAHL duh GORZH]*

At the pharmacy

In the continuity of this chapter, we will try to get you prepared for every scenario. In case you have to go to a pharmacy in a French-speaking country, it's important to know some phrases that will help you communicate your concerns clearly. Although, the system is the same worldwide, you'll need to know the following phrases and words:

English	French	Pronunciation
I've got a prescription here from the doctor	**J'ai une ordonnance du médecin.**	*[ZHAY ewn or-do-NAHNS dew may-ZAN]*
Have you got anything for ___?	**Avez-vous quelque chose pour ___?**	*[ah-VAY voo kel-kuh SHOHZ poor ___?]*
Can you recommend anything for ___?	**Pouvez-vous me recommander quelque chose pour ___?**	*[poo-VAY voo muh ruh-ko-mahn-DAY kel-kuh SHOHZ poor ___?]*
I'm suffering from ___	**Je souffre de ___**	*[zhuh SOOF-ruh duh ___]*
I would like to get this medication	**Je voudrais prendre ce médicament**	*[zhuh voo-DRAY prahndr suh may-dee-ka-MAHN]*
Take one tablet every four hours	**Prenez un comprimé toutes les quatre heures**	*[pruh-NAY ehn kom-pree-MAY toot lay KA-truh UR]*
I feel weak, could you measure my blood pressure?	**Je me sens faible, pouvez-vous mesurer ma tension artérielle ?**	*[zhuh muh SAHN febluh, poo-VAY voo muh-zoo-RAY mah tahn-SYOHN ar-tay-ree-ELL?]*

English	French	Pronunciation
How much is the prescription charge?	**Combien coûte l'ordonnance ?**	*[kohm-BYAN koot lor-do-NAHNS?]*
I have lost the pills I normally take, do you have ___?	**J'ai perdu les comprimés que je prends normalement, avez-vous ___?**	*[ZHAY pair-DU lay kom-pree-MAY kuh zhuh prahn nor-mahl-MAHN, ah-VAY voo ___?]*
You need a doctor's prescription for the medicine	**Vous avez besoin d'une ordonnance du médecin pour le médicament.**	*[vooz ah-VAY buh-ZWAN d'ewn or-do-NAHNS dew may-ZAN poor luh may-dee-ka-MAHN]*
May I please see your health insurance card?	**Puis-je voir votre carte d'assurance maladie ?**	*[pwee zhuh vwar VOTR kart da-soo-RANS mah-lah-DEE?]*
This drug is a suppository. Don't take it orally	**Ce médicament est un suppositoire. Ne le prenez pas par voie orale**	*[suh may-dee-ka-MAHN et ehn soo-po-zee-TWAHR. nuh luh pruh-NAY pah par vwah oh-RAHL]*

English	French	Pronunciation
Pregnancy test	**Un test de grossesse**	*[uhn TEST duh grow-SES]*
Pain relief	**Un antidouleur**	*[uhn AHN-tee doo-LUHR]*
Cough medicine	**Un médicament contre la toux**	*[uhn meh-dee-kah-MAHN KON-truh lah TOO]*
Prescription	**Une prescription/ Une ordonnance**	*[ewn pree-skreep-SYON / ewn ohr-doh-NONS]*
Generic	**Générique**	*[zhay-nay-REEK]*
Brand name	**Un nom de marque**	*[uhn NOHN duh MARK]*
Medication	**Un médicament**	*[uhn meh-dee-kah-MAHN]*
Pill	**Une pilule**	*[ewn pee-LUHL]*
Tablet	**Un comprimé**	*[uhn kohm-pree-MAY]*
Dosage	**Un dosage/ La posologie**	*[uhn doh-ZAHZH / lah poh-so-loh-ZHEE]*
Side effects	**Des effets secondaires**	*[day ZAY-fay soh-GON-dair]*
Anti-diabetic drug	**Un médicament antidiabétique**	*[uhn meh-dee-kah-MAHN ahn-tee-dyah-bay-TEEK]*

Complaints & emergencies

As we established in this chapter, traveling can be quite unpredictable. This is why it's crucial to familiarize yourself with these phrases for voicing your concerns or handling emergencies.

English	French	Pronunciation
I'm lost	Je suis perdu	[zhuh SWEE pair-DOO]
I need to use the toilet	Je dois aller aux toilettes	[zhuh DWAH ah-LAY oh twah-LET]
I can't find my phone	Je ne trouve pas mon téléphone	[zhuh nuh TROOV pah mohn tay-lay-FOHN]
I can't find my wallet	Je ne trouve pas mon portefeuille	[zhuh nuh TROOV pah mohn por-TUH-fuy]
It's too loud	C'est trop bruyant	[say TROH brwee-YAHN]
It's too dirty	C'est trop sale	[say TROH sahl]
I can't afford this	Je ne peux pas me le permettre	[zhuh nuh puh pah muh luh pair-METR]
Please leave me alone	S'il vous plaît, laissez-moi tranquille	[seel voo PLAY, lay-SAY mwah trahn-KEEL]
Go away	Va-t'en / Allez-vous-en	[vah-TAHN / ah-LAY voo-ZAHN]
Help	À l'aide	[ah LED]
Fire	Feu	[fuh]
Fire !	Au feu	[oh FUH]
Call an ambulance	Appelez une ambulance	[ahp-LAY oon ahm-byoo-LAHNS]
Call the police	Appelez la police	[ahp-LAY lah poh-LEES]
Thief	Un voleur	[uhn voh-LUHR]
Someone is following me	Quelqu'un me suit	[kel-KAN muh SWEE]
There's been an accident	Il y a eu un accident	[eel yah uh uhn ahk-see-DAHN]
I'm injured	Je suis blessé	[zhuh SWEE blay-SAY]

SECTION III:
SHORT STORIES

In this section, we'll try to introduce new words and expressions in a fun way, through different short stories. We believe that learning a new language should be an entertaining experience, and the French language is way easier when it's introduced in this way. We'll gradually increase the level of the vocabulary and the tenses used while keeping it adequate for beginners. We encourage you to read the stories as often as needed to get comfortable with the language. The vocabulary words are explained at the end of each story. This will clear up any confusion you may have had and provide you with the tools to progress. You can use these stories to practice reading or writing in French.

Now that it's all clear, let's continue our journey!

STORY #1 LA NOUVELLE MAISON

C'est le grand jour. L'appartement **est vide** et la voiture est **pleine. Tout le monde est prêt, mais Samuel pleure.** Sa mère lui demande :

"Pourquoi tu ne veux **pas partir** ?"

"C'est ma maison. Je veux **rester** ici," dit le petit garçon tout triste.

"Mais cet appartement est trop petit. Je n'aime pas notre **cuisine. Le frigo** est contre le four, il n'y a pas de place pour ranger **la vaisselle** et **les placards** sont très bas. Et ton père n'a pas de **bureau.** Il doit **travailler** dans **le salon** sur ce vieux **fauteuil** ! Et toi? Tu n'aimerais pas avoir une maison plus grande ?," dit la maman.

"Non ! Mes amis **habitent** ici ! J'aime beaucoup cette maison. Je ne veux pas partir !"

"D'accord, Samuel, nous allons à la nouvelle maison maintenant. Si elle ne te plaît pas, **nous reviendrons** ici, d'accord ?," dit la maman.

"Oui, c'est bon !," répond Samuel.

Plus tard, la famille arrive à la nouvelle maison. Samuel est très excité et **court dans le jardin.** Il y a **une jolie balançoire, des arbres** et des rangs de fleurs. C'est un jardin vraiment agréable. Il dit alors :

"Maman, **regarde, je peux jouer** ici et je peux même avoir **un chien** !"

Samuel, ses parents et sa sœur Angèle entrent dans la maison. **Les meubles** sont bien décorés. La cuisine est beaucoup plus grande. Il y a une belle table en bois avec quatre chaises et **la cuisinière** est entièrement neuve. **La salle de bain** est aussi bien plus jolie, avec **une douche** mais aussi **une grande baignoire !**

Samuel monte **les escaliers** et s'exclame :

"J'adore cette maison ! Et j'ai enfin **une chambre** pour moi ! Maintenant je peux ranger tous **mes jouets et dormir** sans **ma sœur !**"

La mère dit à Angèle :

"Regarde ton **frère** ! Il était **triste,** mais maintenant il est tout **joyeux.**"

STORY #1 THE NEW HOUSE

It's the big day. The apartment is **empty,** and the car is **full. Everyone** is **ready,** but Samuel **is crying.** His mother asks him:

"Why don't you want **to leave**?"

"This is my home. I want **to stay** here," says the sad little boy.

"But this apartment is too small. I don't like our **kitchen**. The **fridge** is against the **oven,** there's no room to put the **dishes,** and the **cupboards** are very low. And your father doesn't have an **office**. He has **to work** in the **living room** on that old **armchair**! And what about you? Wouldn't you like a bigger house?" says the mom.

"No! My friends **live** here! I really like this house. I don't want to leave it!"

"Okay, Samuel, we're going to the new house now. If you don't like it, we'll **come back** here, okay?" says the mom.

"Yes, that's fine!" replies Samuel.

Later, the family arrives at the new house. Samuel is very excited and **runs** into the **garden**. There's a lovely **swing, trees,** and rows of flowers. It's a beautiful garden. Then he says:

"Mommy, **look**, I can **play** here and I can even have **a dog**!"

Samuel, his parents and his sister Angèle enter the house. **The furniture** is beautifully arranged. The kitchen is much bigger. There's a nice wooden table with four chairs, and the **stove** is brand new. The **bathroom** is also much nicer, with a **shower** and a large **bathtub**!

Samuel climbs **the stairs** and shouts:

"I love this house! And I finally have **a bedroom** of my own! Now I can keep all my **toys** and **sleep** without my **sister**!

The mother says to Angèle:

"Look at your **brother**! He was so **sad,** but now he's all **cheerful**."

English	French	Pronunciation
Empty	Vide	[VEED]
Full	Plein(e)	[PLEHN] (for masculine) / [PLEHN] (for feminine)
Everyone	Tout le monde	[TOO luh MOND]
Ready	Prêt(e)	[PREH] (for masculine) / [PREHT] (for feminine)
To cry	Pleurer	[PLUH-ray]
To leave	Partir	[PAR-teer]
To stay	Rester	[RES-tay]
The kitchen	La cuisine	[lah kwee-ZEEN]
A fridge	Un frigo	[uhn FREE-goh]
An oven	Un four	[uhn FOOR]
The dishes	La vaisselle	[lah vay-SEL]
A cupboard	Un placard	[uhn PLAH-kar]
An office	Un bureau	[uhn boo-ROH]
To work	Travailler	[trah-vah-YAY]
The living room	Le salon	[luh sah-LON]
An armchair	Un fauteuil	[uhn foh-TOY]
To live	Habiter	[ah-bee-TAY]
To come (to come back)	Venir (revenir)	[vuh-NEER] / [ruh-vuh-NEER]
The garden	Le jardin	[luh zhar-DAN]
To run	Courir	[koo-REER]
A swing	Une balançoire	[oon bah-lahn-SWAR]
A tree	Un arbre	[uhn AR-bruh]
To look at	Regarder	[ruh-gar-DAY]
To play	Jouer	[zhoo-AY]
A dog	Un chien	[uhn SHYAN]
The furniture	Les meubles	[lay MUHB-luh]
A stove	Une cuisinière	[oon kwee-zee-NYARE]
The stairs	Les escaliers	[lay es-kah-LYAY]
The bathroom	La salle de bain	[lah sal duh BAN]
A shower	Une douche	[oon DOOSH]
A bathtub	Une baignoire	[oon ben-WAR]
The bedroom	La chambre	[lah SHOM-bruh]

Speak Abroad
Academy

English	French	Pronunciation
A toy	**Un jouet**	[uhn zhoo-AY]
To sleep	**Dormir**	[dor-MEER]
A brother / A sister	**Un frère / Une soeur**	[uhn FREHR] / [oon SUHR]
Cheerful	**Joyeux (joyeuse)**	[zhwah-YUH] (masc.) / [zhwah-YUHZ] (fem.)
Sad	**Triste**	[TREEST]

A. **It's not usually easy for kids to move to a new house but as the story demonstrated, it does eventually get easier. Based on the text, carefully answer the following questions in French**

Hint: Quel = Which

1.   Which piece of furniture in the apartment is quite old?
2.   Where is the fridge in the kitchen?
3.   What kind of pet can Samuel now have in his new home ?
4.   What can you find in the garden ?
5.   What things is Samuel now able to put in his room?

B. **What would be the best choice to complete these sentences?**

1.   Samuel ne veut pas partir parce que _____ habitent ici.
     a) ses amis   b) ses grand-parents
2.   La cuisine dans l'ancien appartement est _____.
     a) trop petite   b) trop moche
3.   Samuel est excité en arrivant à la nouvelle maison et court _____.
     a) dans la cuisine   b) dans le jardin
4.   La nouvelle salle de bain a une douche et _____.
     a) une balançoire   b) une baignoire
5.   Samuel est content car il peut enfin _____.
     a) dormir sans sa sœur   b) dormir avec ses parents

STORY #2 LE MALENTENDU

Peter est un **jeune ingénieur** dans une importante **entreprise privée**. Il **se lève** tous les jours **très tôt** le matin et il passe la journée dans un petit bureau à travailler devant son **ordinateur**. C'est **un métier** difficile et stressant. Après une longue journée de travail, il aime aller au bar pour pour **manger des frites** et **se reposer**. Ce mercredi, il **commande** une **bière** et une **assiette** de frites avant de **s'asseoir** à une table commune.

Pendant qu'il mange, il **regarde** une vidéo **amusante** sur son téléphone. Peter adore les vidéos avec des animaux **mignons**, surtout les chats. Soudain, **il s'arrête de rire**. Il y a une main sur son assiette. L'inconnu à droite de Peter lit **un journal** et met une frite dans sa bouche.

Peter est surpris et pense : "C'est **peut-être une erreur**." Mais l'inconnu mange encore une frite dans la **même** assiette. Peter est **en colère**. "Mais c'est incroyable ! Cet homme mange dans mon assiette !"

Peter mange alors **davantage** de frites. Il mange vite et il ne peut pas **se concentrer sur** sa vidéo. Mais l'inconnu ne le regarde pas. Il continue de lire son journal et de manger ses frites.

Peter regarde l'assiette. "**Il ne reste que cinq frites** ! Je **déteste** ça."

Soudain, l'étranger mange les cinq **dernières** frites ! L'assiette est vide. Peter est furieux. Il se lève, mais tout d'un coup il **voit** deux assiettes sur la table. L'assiette devant l'inconnu est vide. Et l'assiette devant Peter est pleine de frites.

Alors, Peter se rend compte de son erreur : "Oh non. J'ai mangé les frites de cet homme !" pense Peter. Il est vraiment **gêné** et il ne sait pas comment **s'excuser**.

Confus mais calme, l'inconnu regarde maintenant Peter.

"Tout va bien ? Je peux vous **aider** ?," demande l'inconnu.

Peter **sourit** puis dit :

"Excusez-moi, monsieur. Voulez-vous **partager** mes frites ?"

Speak Abroad
Academy

STORY #2 THE MISUNDERSTANDING

Peter is a **young engineer** at a large **private company**. He **gets up very early** every day and spends his time in a small office working in front of his **computer**. It's a tough, stressful job. So, after a long day's work, he likes to go to the bar **to eat French fries** and **relax**. This Wednesday, he **orders a beer** and **a plate** of fries and **sits down** at a shared table.

While he eats, he **watches** a **funny** video on his phone. Peter loves videos with **cute** animals, especially cats. Suddenly, he **stops laughing**. There's **a hand** reaching onto his plate. **The stranger** to Peter's right is reading **a newspaper** and putting a French fry in his **mouth**.

Peter is surprised and thinks, "**Maybe** this is **a mistake**." But the stranger eats another fry from the **same** plate. This time, Peter gets **angry**. "This is unbelievable! This man is eating from my plate!"

Peter then starts to eat **more** fries. He's eating fast and can't **focus on** his video. But the stranger doesn't look at him. He continues to read his newspaper and eat fries off the plate.

Peter looks at the plate. "**There are only five fries left!** I **can't stand** it."

Suddenly, the stranger eats the **last** five fries! The plate is empty. Peter is furious. He gets up, but suddenly **sees** two plates on the table. The plate in front of the stranger is empty. And the plate in front of Peter is full of French fries.

Then Peter realizes his mistake: "Oh no. I ate that man's fries!" thinks Peter. He's really **embarrassed** and has no idea how to **apologize**.

Confused but calm, the stranger now looks at Peter.

"Are you alright? Can I **help** you?" the stranger asks.

Peter **smiles**, then says:

"Excuse me, sir. **Would you like to share** my fries?"

English	French	Pronunciation
Young	Jeune	[zhuhn]
An engineer	Un ingénieur	[uhn an-zhay-NYUHR]
A private company	Une entreprise privée	[ewn ahn-truh-PREEZ pree-VAY]
To stand up/ To get up	Se lever	[suh luh-VAY]
Very early	Très tôt	[TRAY toh]
A computer	Un ordinateur	[uhn or-dee-na-TUHR]
A job	Un métier	[uhn may-TYAY]
To eat (ate)	Manger (past. mangé)	(past. mangé) [mahn-ZHAY]
French fries	Des frites (f)	[day FREET]
To relax	Se reposer	[suh ruh-poh-ZAY]
To order	Commander	[koh-mahn-DAY]
A beer	Une bière	[ewn byehr]
A plate of (french fries)	Une assiette de (frites)	[ewn ah-SYET duh FREET]
To sit down	S'asseoir	[sa-SWAHR]
To watch (a video)	Regarder (une vidéo)	[ruh-gahr-DAY (ewn vee-day-oh)]
Funny	Amusant(e)	[ah-mew-ZAHN(t)]
Cute	Mignon (ne)	[mee-NYAWN(nuh)]
To stop doing something	S'arrêter de + INFINITIVE	[sah-RAY-tay duh]
To laugh	Rire	[REER]
The hand	La main	[lah mahN]
A stranger	Un inconnu	[uhn an-koh-NEW]
A newspaper	Un journal	[uhn zhoor-NAHL]
A mouth	Une bouche	[ewn boosh]
Maybe	Peut-être	[puh-TAY-truh]
A mistake	Une erreur	[ewn ay-RUHR]
The same	Le (la) même	[luh (lah) MEM]
Angry	En colère	[ahn koh-LAIR]
More	Davantage	[dah-vahn-TAHZH]
To focus on	Se concentrer sur	[suh kohn-sahn-TRAY sur]
There's only _____ left	Il ne reste que _____	[eel nuh REHST kuh]
To hate/ Can't stand	Détester	[day-TESS-tay]
Last	Dernier (dernière)	[DAIR-nyay (DAIR-nyair)]
To see	Voir	[vwahr]

English	French	Pronunciation
Embarrassed	**Gêné(e)**	*[zhay-NAY]*
To apologize	**S'excuser**	*[seks-kew-ZAY]*
To help	**Aider**	*[ay-DAY]*
To smile	**Sourire**	*[soo-REER]*
Would you like to...	**Voulez-vous + INFINITIVE**	*[voo-LAY voo]*
To share	**Partager**	*[par-tah-ZHAY]*

A. **Based on the text, carefully answer the following questions in French:**

1. What is Peter's job?
2. Peter spends his day working in front of what?
3. What is Peter watching on his phone while eating?
4. What is the stranger sitting to Peter's right reading?

B. **Complete the sentence in French with the correct details from the story.**

Peter est un jeune _____. Il travaille tous les jours devant son _____.

Peter est _____ parce que l'inconnu mange ses frites. C'est une erreur parce qu'il y a deux _____ de frites sur la table.

C. **Did you pay attention to the story? All these sentences are incorrect. Can you correct them using specific details from the story?**

1. L'histoire se passe un jeudi.
2. Peter aime regarder des vidéos tristes.
3. L'inconnu est assis à gauche de Peter.
4. Peter a mangé les 5 dernières frites.

STORY #3 L'ANIMAL DE COMPAGNIE

François et sa **femme** Céline sont des jeunes mariés qui viennent de s'installer dans leur nouvelle maison.. Elle est très belle, avec un grand jardin et des murs joliment décorés. **Cependant**, même si la maison a plusieurs chambres, ils n'ont pas d'**enfants**. Alors, ils **sont d'accord** pour adopter leur **premier animal de compagnie**.

François dit:

> "**Chérie**, je pense que ce serait une bonne idée d'avoir un gros **chien** pour garder notre maison !"

> "**Hors de question !**" répond son épouse. Les chiens mangent beaucoup et ils **sentent mauvais**. Il nous faut un animal plus petit et qui coûte moins cher à **nourrir**. J'aimerais avoir **un chat**. Un chat, c'est petit, propre et **mignon**."

> "Non, je ne suis pas d'accord. Les chats sont **ennuyeux**. Ils dorment tout le temps. Et quand ils **se réveillent**, ils courent partout et ils **griffent** les meubles. A mon avis, Les chiens sont beaucoup **plus gentils**", dit le mari.

> Céline n'est pas contente. Mais pour l'instant, elle attend de voir ce que **le magasin** peut leur proposer. "**Allons** à **l'animalerie** pour choisir **ensemble**," dit Céline.

L'animalerie se trouve dans le centre-ville. Ils garent **la voiture** dans la rue à côté et entrent dans le magasin. **A l'intérieur**, il y a beaucoup d'animaux différents. Des **lapins**, des cochons d'Inde, **des oiseaux**, des lézards, et bien sûr des chiens et des petits chats. Céline admire un chaton qui dort, il est tout noir avec des petites **pattes**. Il ouvre **lentement** ses beaux **yeux** bleus.

Quand il voit le chaton, son mari dit:

> "Tu vois, je te l'avais dit ! Il est trop **paresseux** ! Il va dormir toute la journée et il va venir vers nous juste pour manger."

François regarde dans la boutique et il trouve un petit chiot brun avec des yeux noirs.

> "Regarde ! Il est adorable ! Est-ce que tu veux le **caresser** ?"

> "Ah non, regarde sa salive ! Il est dégoûtant !" répond Céline.

> "Mais au moins il est **utile** et il est beaucoup plus mignon que ce chat," répond le mari.

> "Non, **tu as tort**. Le chat est plus mignon. Et il dort comme un petit ange," dit l'épouse.

Ils commencent à **se disputer** et **le vendeur** leur dit :

> "Madame, monsieur, je vois que vous ne savez pas quel animal choisir. Alorsvenez voir ce **perroquet**, je vous prie. Je pense qu'il va **résoudre** tous vos problèmes."

Il leur montre un oiseau très beau avec des **plumes** bleues et vertes, de grandes **ailes**, un long **bec** et des petits yeux.

Céline dit:

"Oh, comme il est beau, je le veux à la maison !"

"**Moi aussi** ! Je vais lui **apprendre** à dire quelques **phrases**."

Céline et François sont ravis. Ils paient le commerçant et sortent de l'animalerie.

Céline dit à l'oiseau:

"Alors, **comment ça va**, mon petit Coco ?"

"Coco ? Non, il s'appellera Ron," répond le mari.

"Je ne veux pas encore me disputer avec toi maintenant," répond Céline.

François regarde sa femme dans les yeux et **sourit** gentiment. Elle se met à rire.

Ils sont d'accord pour appeler leur perroquet Ron-Coco et **marchent** ensemble la **main dans la main**.

STORY #3 THE PET

François and his **wife** Céline are a young married couple who have recently moved into their new home. It's a lovely house, with a large garden and beautifully decorated walls. **However**, even though the house has several bedrooms, they don't have any **children**. So they **agree** to adopt their **first pet**.

François says:

> "**Honey**, I think it would be a good idea to have a big **dog** to guard our house!"

> "'**Absolutely not!**" replies his wife. "Dogs eat a lot and they **smell bad**. What we need is a smaller animal that costs less **to feed**. I'd prefer to have **a cat**. A cat is small, clean and **cute**."

> "No, I don't agree. Cats are **boring**. They sleep all the time. And when they **wake up**, they run around and **scratch** the furniture. In my opinion, dogs are much **nicer**," says the **husband**.

> Céline is not happy. But for now, the best thing to do is to see what **the store** can do for them. "**Let's go to the pet shop** and choose **together**," says Céline.

The pet shop is in the center of town. They park **the car** in the street nearby and walk into the store. **Inside**, there are lots of different animals. **Rabbits**, guinea pigs, **birds**, lizards, and of course dogs and kittens. Céline is delighted to see a kitten lying asleep, all black with little **paws**. He **slowly** opens his beautiful blue **eyes**.

When he sees the kitten, her husband says:

> "See, I told you so! He's so **lazy!** He's going to sleep all day and then he'll come to us just to eat."

François checks in the store and finds a little brown puppy with black eyes.

> "Look! He's so adorable! Would you like to **pet** him?"

> "Ah no, look at his saliva! He's disgusting!" replies Céline.

> "But at least he's **useful** and he's much cuter than that cat" replies the husband.

> "No, **you're wrong**. The cat is cuter. And he sleeps like a little angel," says the wife.

They start **arguing** and the **salesman** says:

> "Madam, sir, I see you don't know which animal to choose. So, please, come and see this **parrot**. I think it will **solve** all your problems."

He shows them a beautiful bird with blue and green **feathers**, big **wings**, a long **beak** and small eyes.

Céline says:

"Oh, how beautiful he is, I want him in our house!"

"**Me too**! I'm going to **teach** him to say a few **sentences**."

Céline and François are delighted. They pay the shopkeeper and leave the pet shop.

Céline says to the bird:

"So, **how are you**, my little Coco?"

"Coco? No, he'll be called Ron," replies the husband.

"I don't want to argue with you again now," replies Céline.

François looks his wife in the eye and smiles gently. She starts laughing. They agree to call their parrot Ron-Coco and walk together **holding hands**.

English	French	Pronunciation
A wife/spouse	**Une femme/ une épouse**	*[ewn FAHM/ewn ay-POOZ]*
A husband/spouse	**Un mari/ un époux**	*[uh MAR-ee/uh nay-POO]*
A child / children	**Un enfant / des enfants**	*[uh naw-FAHN/day naw-FAHN]*
To agree	**Être d'accord**	*[eh-truh da-KOR]*
First	**Premier (première)**	*[pruh-MYAY/pruh-MYER]*
A pet	**Un animal de compagnie**	*[uh nah-nee-MAHL duh kom-pah-NYEE]*
Honey / Darling	**Chéri(e)**	*[shay-REE/shay-REE]*
A dog / A puppy	**Un chien / Un chiot**	*[uh SHYEN/uh shee-OH]*
Absolutely not!	**Hors de question !**	*[or duh KES-tyon]*
To smell bad	**Sentir mauvais**	*sawn-TEER moh-VAY]*
To feed	**Nourrir**	*[noo-REER]*
A cat / A kitten	**Un chat / Un chaton**	*[uh SHAH/uh shah-TON]*
Cute	**Mignon(ne)**	*[meen-YON/meen-YON]*
Boring	**Ennuyeux(euse)**	*[awn-wee-YEU/awn-wee-YUHZ]*
To wake up	**Se réveiller**	*[suh ray-vay-YAY]*
To scratch	**Griffer**	*[gree-FAY]*
Nice	**Gentil(le)**	*[zhawn-TEE/zhawn-TEE]*
A store	**Un magasin**	*[uh mah-gah-ZAN]*
Let's go to ___	**Allons à ___**	*[ah-LAWNZ ah ___]*
Together	**Ensemble**	*[awn-SAHMBL]*
A pet shop	**Une animalerie**	*[ewn ah-nee-mah-luh-REE]*
A car	**Une voiture**	*[ewn vwha-TYOOR]*
Inside	**A l'intérieur**	*[ah la(n)-tay-ree-YUR]*
A rabbit	**Un lapin**	*[uh lah-PA(N)]*
A bird	**Un oiseau**	*[uh(n) wah-ZOH]*
The paws	**Les pattes**	*[lay PAHT]*
Slowly	**Lentement**	*[lah(n)-tuh-MAWN]*
An eye / Eyes	**Un oeil / Des yeux**	*[uh(n) UY/deh ZYEU]*
Lazy	**Paresseux (se)**	*[pah-ray-SUH/pah-ray-SUHZ]*
To pet (an animal)	**Caresser**	*[kah-ray-SAY]*
Useful	**Utile**	*[ew-TEEL]*
You're right / wrong	**Tu as raison / tort**	*[tyoo ah ray-ZAW/tyoo ah TOR]*

English	French	Pronunciation
A salesperson	Un vendeur/une vendeuse	[uh(n) vawn-DUHR/ ewn vawn-DEUHZ]
To argue	Se disputer	[suh dee-spoo-TAY]
To solve	Résoudre	[ray-ZOO-druh]
A parrot	Un perroquet	[uh(n) peh-roh-KAY]
The beak	Le bec	[luh BEK]
The wings	Les ailes	[lay ZEL]
The feathers	Les plumes	[lay PLOOM]
Me too	Moi aussi	[mwah oh-SEE]
To teach	Apprendre	[ah-PRON-druh]
A sentence	Une phrase	[ewn FRAWZ]
How are you?	Comment ça va ?	[koh-MAWN sah VAH]
To walk	Marcher	[mar-SHAY]
Holding hands	Main dans la main	[man daw(n) lah MAN]

A. **Do you like animals? These two clearly do. At least as much as they like arguing... What happened in the story? Please answer all the questions in French.**

1. Why does François want to adopt a big dog?
2. What reasons does Céline give for preferring a cat over a dog?
3. How does François describe cats when he sees the black kitten at the pet shop?
4. What does the salesman suggest when François and Céline can't agree on which pet to adopt?

B. **Based on your understanding of the story, can you determine whether these sentences are right or wrong?**

1. François et Céline sont frère et sœur – Vrai / Faux
2. François pense que le petit chat va beaucoup dormir – Vrai / Faux
3. Le perroquet est très beau avec des plumes vertes et de petites ailes – Vrai / Faux
4. François et Céline sont d'accord pour appeler leur oiseau Coco – Vrai / Faux

C. **According to the story, which words would you choose to complete these sentences?**

1. François veut adopter un _____ pour garder la maison.
2. Céline préfère adopter un _____ parce qu'ils sont petits, propres et mignons.

STORY #4 UNE JOURNÉE À LA PLAGE

C'est **l'été**. Emmanuel et son ami Lucas sont en vacances en Italie, dans une ville magnifique. Ils adorent découvrir la cuisine locale et apprennent même quelques mots d'italien pour parler avec **les gens** dans les restaurants et à l'hôtel. **Aujourd'hui**, ils profitent du beau **temps** pour aller à **la plage**. Alors, après **le petit-déjeuner**, ils partent en voiture.

Dans **la voiture**, ils admirent **le paysage**. **Le soleil brille**. **Les collines** sont grandes et vertes. Il y a des fleurs roses et jaunes **partout**.

"Quelle **chance** ! Ça va vraiment être une journée magnifique," pense Emmanuel.

"Quel temps superbe !" pense Lucas.

Dix minutes plus tard, ils arrivent près de la plage. Ils garent la voiture, prennent leurs **serviettes** et leurs **maillots de bain**, et courent vers la plage tout excités. Malheureusement, ils sont vite **déçus**. La plage est **bondée**. En plus, les gens jouent de la musique très **fort**. Les enfants courent partout. Il y a des bébés qui pleurent ! Pour les deux amis, c'est un désastre.

"Regarde le monde qu'il y a !" dit Lucas.

"Oui, et ils sont très **bruyants** !" répond Emmanuel.

Ils trouvent une place et s'assoient à côté d'une petite famille. C'est **le seul** espace **libre**. Les enfants font des **châteaux de sable**. Les parents dorment.

"**Au moins**, nous sommes près de l'eau", dit Emmanuel.

"Oui, et l'océan est magnifique", dit Lucas.

Lucas et Emmanuel **essaient de se détendre**. Mais quelques minutes plus tard, un enfant **jette du sable** sur Lucas. Un autre jette de **l'eau** sur Emmanuel.

"**Arrêtez ça** ! S'il vous plaît !" dit Lucas, qui commence à être en colère.

Mais les enfants rient et continuent. Les parents **s'en moquent** et font semblant de ne pas **entendre**. Emmanuel **en a assez**.

"Viens, **on rentre** !", dit-il.

"Non, pas encore", répond Lucas.

"Mais ces enfants sont des monstres !" s'exclame Emmanuel, en colère.

Lucas regarde de l'autre côté de la plage.

"**Là-bas**, je suis sûr que c'est plus **tranquille**."

"Bon, d'accord," dit Emmanuel.

Emmanuel et Lucas marchent sur la plage bondée pendant dix minutes. Il y a beaucoup moins de monde maintenant, et c'est plus agréable.

De l'autre côté de la plage, tout est calme et ils sont seuls. Ils regardent la mer et les oiseaux. Ils **nagent** dans **la mer**. L'eau est **froide**, mais ils sont heureux. Ils **trouvent** même de beaux **coquillages** qu'ils vont garder en souvenir.

Une heure plus tard, Emmanuel demande :

"Lucas, tu sais comment revenir à la voiture ?"

"**Je ne sais pas**, **mais on verra plus tard**. C'est une magnifique journée et il faut en profiter !" répond Lucas en riant.

"Tu as raison", dit Emmanuel.

Pour l'instant, la plage est calme et le soleil brille toujours. Parfois, **on a juste besoin de fermer les yeux** et de se détendre.

STORY #4 A DAY AT THE BEACH

It's **summertime**. Emmanuel and his friend Lucas are on vacation in a beautiful Italian town. They love discovering the local cuisine and are even learning a few words of Italian to talk to **people** in restaurants and hotels.

Today, they're taking advantage of the beautiful **weather** to go to **the beach**. So, after **breakfast**, they drive off.

In **the car**, they admire **the scenery. The sun is shining. The hills** are big and green. There are pink and yellow flowers **everywhere**.

> "How **lucky** we are! It's really going to be a wonderful day," thinks Emmanuel.

> "The weather's just perfect," thinks Lucas.

Ten minutes later, they arrive near the beach. They park the car, grab their **towels** and **swimsuits**, and run down to the beach, full of excitement.

Unfortunately, they are quickly **disappointed**. The beach is **crowded**. On top of that, people are playing **loud** music. Children are running everywhere. Babies are crying! For the two friends, it's a real disaster.

> "Look at how crowded it is!" says Lucas.

> "Yes, and they're so **loud**!" replies Emmanuel.

They find a spot and sit down next to a small family. It's **the only free** spot left. The children are making **sandcastles**. The parents are asleep.

> "**At least** we're near the water," says Emmanuel.

> "Yes, and the ocean is gorgeous," says Lucas.

Lucas and Emmanuel **try to relax**. But after a few minutes, a child **throws sand** at Lucas. Another throws **water** at Emmanuel.

> "**Stop that**! Please!" says Lucas, who's starting to get angry.

But the kids laugh and carry on. The parents **don't seem to care** and pretend not **to hear**. Emmanuel **has had enough**.

> "Come on, **let's go home**!" he says.

> "No, not yet," replies Lucas.

> "But these kids are monsters!" shouts Emmanuel angrily.

Lucas looks across the beach.

"**Over there**, I'm sure it's **quieter**."

"Well, okay," says Emmanuel.

Emmanuel and Lucas walk along the crowded beach for ten minutes. There are far fewer people now, and it's more pleasant.

On the other side of the beach, it's quiet, and they're alone. They contemplate the sea and the birds. They **swim** in **the sea**. The water is **cold**, but they're happy. They even **find** some beautiful **shells** to keep as souvenirs.

An hour later, Emmanuel asks:

"Lucas, do you know how to get back to the car?"

"**I don't**, but **we'll figure it out later**. It's a lovely day and we've got to make the most of it!" replies Lucas, laughing.

"You're right," says Emmanuel.

For now, the beach is peaceful and the sun is still shining. Sometimes, **you just need to close your eyes** and relax.

English	French	Pronunciation
Summer	L'été	[LAY-tay]
People	Les gens	[LAY zhahn]
Today	Aujourd'hui	[oh-ZHOOR-dwee]
The weather	Le temps/la météo	[luh TAHN] / [lah may-TAY-oh]
The beach	La plage	[lah PLAHZH]
Breakfast	Le petit-déjeuner	[luh puh-TEE day-zhuh-NAY]
A car	Une voiture	[ewn vwah-TOOR]
The scenery	Un paysage	[uhN pay-ee-ZAHZH]
The sun	Le soleil	[luh soh-LAY]
To shine	Briller	[bree-YAY]
A hill	Une colline	[ewn koh-LEEN]
Everywhere	Partout	[par-TOO]
Luck	La chance	[lah SHAHNS]
A towel	Une serviette	[ewn sair-VYET]
A swimsuit	Un maillot de bain	[uhN mah-YO duh BAN]
Disappointed	Déçu(e)	[day-SOO]
Crowded	Bondé(e)	[bon-DAY]
Loud (music)	Fort	[FOR] / [FORT]
Noisy/ Loud	Bruyant(e)	[bree-YAHN] / [bree-YANT]
The only	Le seul/ la seule	[luh SUHL] / [lah SUHL]
Free	Libre	[LEE-bruh]
A sandcastle	Un château de sable	[uhN shah-TOH duh SAHBL]
At least	Au moins	[oh MWAN]
To try to	Essayer de	[eh-SAY-yay duh]
To relax	Se détendre	[suh day-TAHNdruh]
Sand	Le sable	[luh SAHBL]
Water	L'eau (f)	[loh]
To throw	Jeter	[zhuh-TAY]
Stop that!	Arrêtez ça !	[ah-RAY-tay sah]
(They) don't seem to care	(Ils) s'en moquent	[sahn MOHK]
To hear	Entendre	[ahn-TAHNdruh]
To have enough	En avoir assez	[ahn ah-VWAH rah-SAY]
Let's go home	On rentre	[ohN rahn-truh]

English	French	Pronunciation
Over there	**Là-bas**	*[lah-BAH]*
Quiet	**Tranquille**	*[trahn-KEEL]*
The other side of	**L'autre côté de**	*[LOH-truh koh-TAY duh]*
The sea	**La mer**	*[lah MARE]*
To swim	**Nager**	*[nah-ZHAY]*
Cold	**Froid(e)**	*[FWAH] / [FWAHD]*
To find	**Trouver**	*[troo-VAY]*
A seashell	**Un coquillage**	*[uhN koh-kee-AHZH]*
I don't know	**Je ne sais pas**	*[zhuh nuh say PAH]*
Let's figure it out later	**On verra plus tard**	*[ohN vay-RAH plew TAR]*
You just need to	**On a juste besoin de**	*[ohN ah zhoost buh-ZWAN duh]*
Open / Close your eyes	**Ouvrir / Fermer les yeux**	*[oo-VREER] / [fair-MAY lay ZYUH]*

A. **Sometimes you just need some peace and quiet. Where did the two friends finally manage to enjoy their holiday? Let's answer the questions in French to find out.**

Hint: Où = Where

1. What are the initial problems Emmanuel and Lucas face when they arrive on the beach?
2. What are the two kids initially making when they sit down next to them ?
3. Why do they decide to go to the other side of the beach soon after ?
4. How would you describe the other side of the beach?
5. What are they bringing back home as souvenirs ?

B. **Which options make the most sense according to the story?**

1. Emmanuel et Lucas sont en vacances dans une belle ville _____.
   a) française   b) italienne
2. Après le petit-déjeuner, ils partent en voiture vers la _____.
   a) montagne   b) mer
3. La plage est _____, avec de la musique forte et beaucoup d'enfants.
   a) vide   b) bondée
4. Lucas et Emmanuel sont vite _____ parce que les enfants leur jettent de l'eau et du sable.
   a) déçus   b) joyeux
5. A la fin, Emmanuel demande à Lucas où est _____
   a) la serviette   b) la voiture

STORY #5 DANS LA CUISINE

Aujourd'hui, Angèle est très contente: elle aide sa maman à préparer **un gâteau**.

Elles sont **toutes les deux** dans la cuisine. Sa mère est devant la table et prépare **la pâte** pour le gâteau. Angèle doit rester assise à côté, mais la petite fille est très excitée. Elle court partout et n'arrête pas de rire.

Sa mère prend du **sucre** en poudre et dit : "D'abord, il faut mettre **une cuillère** de sucre."

Mais Angèle n'écoute pas et met quatre cuillères de sucre.

"Arrête, Angèle !" dit la maman. "**C'est beaucoup trop** de sucre !"

Mais Angèle continue de **s'amuser**. Elle court avec **un bol** et, tout d'un coup, elle **tombe**. Elle **casse** le bol et les trois œufs à l'intérieur.

Sa maman est très en colère. Elle prend **une éponge** et nettoie.

"Ça suffit, Angèle. Va dans ta chambre !"

Angèle pleure. "**Je suis désolée**, maman. Laisse-moi t'aider, s'il te plaît. Je vais **faire plus attention**."

Angèle est maintenant beaucoup plus **sage**. Elle s'assoit calmement et regarde sa mère cuisiner.

Après 30 minutes, la préparation est terminée. La maman met alors le gâteau au **four**. Pendant qu'il cuit, Angèle aide à **laver** les bols.

"Très bien, Angèle, c'est le moment de **couper** le gâteau !" dit sa mère.

Angèle coupe le gâteau avec un petit **couteau** et met une part dans **chaque** assiette.

Quatre parts de gâteau : une pour maman, une pour papa, une pour elle, et une pour son petit frère.

"Tu vois, maman, je peux bien t'aider !"

"Oui, tu as raison, Angèle. Mais si tu **fais encore des bêtises**, **la prochaine fois**, tu mangeras de la salade en dessert !"

STORY #5 IN THE KITCHEN

Today, Angèle is very happy: she's helping her mom bake **a cake**. They're **both** in the kitchen. Her mother is at the table, preparing **the batter** for the cake. Angèle is supposed to stay by her side, but the little girl is very excited. She runs around and can't stop laughing.

Her mother gets some powdered **sugar** and says, "First, you need to add **a spoonful** of sugar."

But Angèle doesn't **listen** and adds four spoonfuls of sugar.

"Stop it, Angèle!" says her mom. "**That's way too much** sugar!"

But Angèle continues **to have fun**. She runs with **a bowl** and suddenly trips and **falls**. She **breaks** the bowl and the three **eggs** inside it.

Her mom is very angry. She grabs **a sponge** and cleans up.

"**That's enough**, Angèle. Go to your room!"

Angèle cries. "**I'm sorry**, Mom. Let me help you, please. I'll **be more careful**."

Angèle is much **calmer** now. She sits quietly and watches her mother cook.

After 30 minutes, the preparation is finished. Mom then puts the cake in **the oven**. While it's baking, Angèle helps **wash** the bowls.

"All right, Angèle, it's time to **cut** the cake!" says her mother.

Angèle cuts the cake with a small **knife** and places a slice on **each** plate.

Four slices of cake: one for Mom, one for Dad, one for herself, and one for her little brother.

"You see, Mom, I can help you!"

"Yes, you're right, Angèle. But if **you're naughty** again, **next time** you'll be eating salad for dessert!"

English	French	Pronunciation
A cake	Un gâteau	[uhn GAH-toh]
Both	Tous / Toutes les deux	[too / toot lay DUH]
The batter	La pâte	[lah PAHT]
Sugar	Sucre	[SOOK-ruh]
First	D'abord	[dah-BOHR]
A spoonful	Une cuillère	[ewn kwee-YAIR]
Too much	Trop	[troh]
To listen	Ecouter	[ay-koo-TAY]
To have fun	S'amuser	[sah-mew-ZAY]
An egg	Un œuf	[uhn UHF]
A bowl	Un bol	[uhn BOHL]
To fall	Tomber	[tohm-BAY]
To break	Casser	[kah-SAY]
A sponge	Une éponge	[ewn ay-POHNJ]
That's enough!	Ça suffit !	[sah sew-FEE]
I'm sorry	Je suis désolé (e)	[zhuh swee day-zoh-LAY]
To be more careful	Faire plus attention	[fehr plew zah-tawn-SYAWN]
Calm (for children)	Sage	[sahzh]
An oven	Un four	[uhn FOOR]
To wash	Laver	[lah-VAY]
To cut (a slice of)	Couper (une part de)	[koo-PAY (ewn PAR duh)]
A knife	Un couteau	[uhn koo-TOH]
Every / each	Chaque	[shahk]
To be naughty	Faire des bêtises	[fehr day bay-TEEZ]
Next time	La prochaine fois	[lah proh-SHEN fwah]

A. **A sweet little girl and her mum are cooking together. Warms your heart doesn't it? Let's see how much you understood the story! Remember to answer all these questions in French!**

1. What are Angèle and her mother doing together?
2. What does Angèle do instead of adding just one spoonful of sugar?
3. What happens when Angèle runs with the bowl?
4. What does Angèle do after the cake is put in the oven?

B. **Based on your understanding of the story, can you determine whether these sentences are right or wrong?**

1. Angèle tombe et casse trois sucres – Vrai / Faux
2. Le petit garçon aide à laver les bols – Vrai / Faux
3. Angèle coupe et sert quatre parts de gâteau. Vrai / Faux

C. **Fill in the blanks for the story to make sense**

1. La maman prend du _____ en poudre et dit : « D'abord, il faut mettre une cuillère. »
2. Après 30 minutes, Maman met le gâteau dans _____.
3. Angèle coupe le gâteau avec un petit _____ et met une part dans chaque assiette.

STORY #6 LE DÎNER DE MARIAGE

Eddy et Pauline préparent leur dîner de mariage. **La fête** est pour **demain**. Qui va s'asseoir à côté de qui ?

Eddy :	Alors, où doit **s'asseoir** Marc ? **Il parle** beaucoup !
Pauline :	Il va s'asseoir à côté de **ma cousine**. Elle est très calme et aime écouter les gens.
Eddy :	C'est **une bonne idée**. Et Aymen ? Il est vraiment **timide en général**.
Pauline :	Mettons-le à côté de Thomas. Il est **extraverti** et adore **inclure** les gens timides.
Eddy :	Et pour **ma tante** Emma ? Elle déteste les mariages et **passe son temps à se moquer** des invités.
Pauline :	Mettons-la à côté de **mon oncle** François. C'est aussi son activité favorite ! Ils vont bien **s'amuser** ensemble.
Eddy :	Tu es parfaite, chérie ! Tu as une solution à tout.
Pauline :	**Bien sûr**, mon chéri !
Eddy :	Maintenant, à nos amis.
Pauline :	Ok. Mon amie Amélie **se sent seule** en ce moment. Elle aimerait trouver un homme gentil.
Eddy :	J'ai la personne parfaite, alors. Valentin, il est aussi très romantique.
Pauline :	J'adore ton idée. Qui nous reste-t-il ?
Eddy :	Il ne nous reste plus que **la famille proche**, mais ce n'est pas un problème.
Pauline :	D'accord. Je t'écoute.
Eddy :	**Je pense que** nos frères et sœurs vont s'asseoir tous ensemble à la grande table.
Pauline :	Tu as raison, **ils s'entendent bien**. Ils vont passer un bon moment.

Tout d'un coup, Pauline est très **inquiète**.

Pauline :	Oh non, nos parents...
Eddy :	Ils doivent s'asseoir ensemble. C'est la tradition.
Pauline :	Oui, mais ma mère adore parler de ses chats.
Eddy :	Et ma mère déteste les chats. Et ton père ?
Pauline :	C'est un fan de sport. Il parle toujours de rugby et de tennis.
Eddy :	Mon père n'aime pas le sport. Il préfère parler de cinéma et d'art.

Eddy sourit à Pauline.

Eddy :	**Ne t'inquiète pas**, ma chérie. Nos parents ont au moins deux choses en commun.
Pauline :	C'est vrai ? **Qu'est-ce que c'est ?**
Eddy :	Tout d'abord, ils nous aiment beaucoup. Ils veulent nous voir heureux.
Pauline :	Tu as raison. Et ensuite ?
Eddy :	Et **surtout**, ce qu'ils aiment le plus... c'est **le champagne** !

STORY #6 THE WEDDING DINNER

Eddy and Pauline are preparing their wedding dinner. The **celebration** is **tomorrow**. Who will sit **next to** whom?

Eddy:	So, where should Marc **sit**? He **talks** a lot!
Pauline:	He'll sit next to **my cousin**. She's very quiet and likes listening to people.
Eddy:	**That's a good idea**. What about Aymen? He's **usually** really **shy**.
Pauline:	Let's put him next to Thomas. He's **outgoing** and loves **including** shy people.
Eddy:	And what about **my aunt** Emma? She hates weddings and **spends her time making fun** of the guests.
Pauline:	Let's seat her next to **my uncle** François. That's his favorite activity too! They'll **have a lot of fun** together.
Eddy:	You're perfect, darling! You've got a solution for everything.
Pauline:	**Of course**, honey!
Eddy:	Now, let's talk about our friends.
Pauline:	Okay. My friend Amélie is **feeling lonely** right now. She'd like to meet a nice guy.
Eddy:	I've got the perfect one, then. Valentin, he's very romantic too.
Pauline:	I love your idea. Who's left?
Eddy:	All that is left is our **close family**, but that's no problem.
Pauline:	Okay, I'm listening.
Eddy:	**I think that** our brothers and sisters should sit together at the main table.
Pauline:	You're right, they **get along** well. They'll have a great time.

Suddenly, Pauline becomes very **worried**.

Pauline:	Oh no, our parents...
Eddy:	They need to sit together. It's tradition.
Pauline:	Yes, but my mother loves talking about her cats.
Eddy:	And my mother hates cats. What about your father?
Pauline:	He's a sports fan. He's always talking about rugby and tennis.
Eddy:	My father doesn't like sports. He prefers talking about cinema and art.

Eddy smiles at Pauline.

Eddy:	**Don't worry**, darling. Our parents have at least two things in common.
Pauline:	Really? **What are they?**
Eddy:	First of all, they love us very much. They want to see us happy.
Pauline:	You're right. And the second?
Eddy:	**Most importantly**, what they love the most... is **champagne**!

English	French	Pronunciation
A party / A celebration	Une fête	[ewn FET]
Tomorrow	Demain	[duh-MAN]
Next to	A côté de	[ah koh-TAY duh]
To sit	S'asseoir	[sah-SWAHR]
To talk (about)	Parler (de)	[par-LAY duh]
A cousin	Un cousin / une cousine	[uhn koo-ZAN / ewn koo-ZEEN]
A good idea	Une bonne idée	[ewn bun ee-DAY]
Shy	Timide	[tee-MEED]
Usually	En général	[ahn zhay-nay-RAHL]
Outgoing	Extraverti(e)	[eks-tra-ver-TEE]
To include	Inclure	[ahn-KLUR]
An aunt / an uncle	Une tante / un oncle	[ewn TAHNT / uhn OHN-kluh]
To make fun of	Se moquer	[suh moh-KAY]
To spend one's time (doing)	Passer son temps (à)	[pa-SAY sohn tahn AH]
Of course	Bien sûr	[byan SEWR]
To have fun	S'amuser	[sah-mew-ZAY]
To feel lonely	Se sentir seul(e)	[suh sahn-TEER suhl]
Close relatives	La famille proche	[lah fah-MEE prosh]
I think that	Je pense que	[zhuh PAHNS kuh]
To get along well	S'entendre bien	[sahn-TAHN-druh byan]
Suddenly	Tout d'un coup	[too dun KOO]
Worried	Inquiet / Inquiète	[ahn-KYAY / ahn-KYET]
Don't worry	Ne t'inquiète pas	[nuh tain-KYET pah]
What is it?	Qu'est-ce que c'est ?	[KESS kuh say]
Most importantly	Surtout	[sewr-TOO]

A. **Deciding who to invite at a wedding dinner is no mean feat! Let's see if you got it right! Remember to answer these questions in French.**

1. Which guest is quite outgoing?
2. Which guest is usually very shy?
3. Which guest hates weddings?
4. Which guests really love to drink champagne ?

B. **So many people are invited but who will be sitting next to whom? Fill in the blanks using specific details from the story.**

1. Marc va s'asseoir à côté de la _____ de Pauline.
2. Aymen va s'asseoir à côté de _____.
3. La tante d'Eddy va s'asseoir à côté de l'_____ de Pauline.
4. Amélie va s'asseoir à côté de _____.

C. **Time to test your understanding! Choose the best word according to the story.**

1. [La mère – la tantem – fille] de Pauline adore parler de ses chats.
2. Le père d'Eddy préfère parler de [sport – cinéma – musique] et d'art.

STORY #7 MANGE TES FRUITS ET TES LÉGUMES!

Tous les jours, Julia a le même problème : son fils Jimmy, qui a quatre ans, n'aime pas manger ses fruits et **légumes**. Julia est assise à la table de la cuisine et regarde Jimmy. Il a l'air **fâché**, et ses bras sont croisés devant son assiette. Jimmy ne veut manger que des **bonbons**, et à chaque **repas**, c'est toujours pareil.

Julia :   Ouvre la bouche !
Jimmy :   Non ! Non !
Julia :   Ce sont des épinards, Jimmy. C'est très bon pour ta **santé** !
Jimmy :   Je n'aime pas les épinards ! Je veux des bonbons !
Julia :   Tu veux un fruit ? Prends une **banane**.
Jimmy :   Non ! Je déteste les bananes, c'est **dégoûtant** !
Julia :   Regarde cette **pastèque** ! Elle est rouge et **juteuse**.
Jimmy :   Non ! Je veux des bonbons ! Je n'aime pas la pastèque.
Julia :   Dans ce cas, voici des **fraises**. Elles sont petites, rouges et **sucrées**, exactement comme les bonbons.
Jimmy :   Non ! Tu **mens**, maman ! Je veux de **vrais** bonbons !

Jimmy **se met à** pleurer. Julia est **fatiguée**. Son mari travaille toute la journée et elle est seule à la maison pour **s'occuper de** leur enfant. Aujourd'hui, c'est encore **pire**. Au menu, il y a du brocoli, des **choux-fleurs** et du **raisin**. Tout ce que Jimmy déteste manger. Julia ne sait pas quoi faire.

Soudain, elle a une nouvelle idée.

Julia :   Regarde Jimmy. Aujourd'hui, c'est différent, ce ne sont pas des fruits et des légumes.
Jimmy :   Je ne comprends pas. C'est quoi, alors ?

Julia prend les raisins.

Julia :   C'est un alien ! Il a huit **têtes**. Il va venir pour tout **détruire** ! Et regarde ça, ce n'est pas du brocoli, c'est **un arbre** magique ! Tu dois le sauver!
Jimmy :   Oh, **comment** je dois faire alors ?
Julia :   Tu dois le **cacher dans ton ventre**.

Jimmy prend alors le brocoli et le mange. Julia est très contente.

Julia :   Maintenant, tu dois détruire l'alien ! Il faut aussi le manger très **vite**.
Jimmy :   D'accord, maman ! Je vais tous vous sauver.

Jimmy prend alors le raisin et le mange.

Soudain, il dit :

Jimmy :   Il y a un gros problème.
Julia :   Qu'est-ce qu'il y a, mon chéri ?
Jimmy :   L'arbre ne peut pas **vivre** dans mon ventre. Il a besoin de **pluie**.

Julia sourit et prend les choux-fleurs.

Julia :   Regarde. Ce sont des **nuages**. Si tu les manges alors l'arbre pourra **boire** l'eau
            de la pluie.
Jimmy :   Oh, c'est parfait ! Je vais sauver l'arbre.

Jimmy mange toute son assiette pour la première fois. Julia est heureuse.

Depuis ce jour, elle lui **raconte des histoires** à chaque repas et Jimmy finit toujours son assiette.

STORY #7 EAT YOUR FRUITS AND VEGETABLES!

Every day, Julia faces the same problem: her four-year-old son, Jimmy, doesn't like to eat his fruits and **vegetables**. Julia is sitting at the kitchen table, watching Jimmy. He looks **upset** and is crossing his arms in front of his plate. Jimmy only wants to eat **sweets**, and at every **meal**, it's always the same story.

Julia: Open your mouth!
Jimmy: No! No!
Julia: It's **spinach**, Jimmy. It's very good for your **health**!
Jimmy: I don't like spinach! I want candy!
Julia: Do you want a piece of fruit? How about a **banana**?
Jimmy: No! I hate bananas, they're **disgusting**!
Julia: Look at this **watermelon**! It's red and **juicy**.
Jimmy: No! I want candy! I don't like watermelon.
Julia: In that case, here are some **strawberries**. They're small, red, and **sweet**, just like candy.
Jimmy: No! You're **lying**, Mom! I want **real** candy!

Jimmy **starts to** cry. Julia feels **exhausted**. Her husband is at work all day, and she's home alone **taking care** of Jimmy. Today, it's even **worse**. On the menu are broccoli, **cauliflower**, and **grapes** — everything Jimmy hates. Julia is at a loss.

Suddenly, she has a new idea.

Julia: Look, Jimmy. Today is different, these aren't fruits and vegetables.
Jimmy: I don't understand. What are they, then?

Julia picks up the grapes.

Julia: It's an alien! It's got eight **heads**, and it's coming to **destroy** everything! And look at this — it's not broccoli, it's a magic **tree**! You've got to **save** it!
Jimmy: Oh, **how** do I do that?
Julia: You have to **hide** it **in your belly**.

Jimmy grabs the broccoli and eats it. Julia is thrilled.

Julia: Now you have to destroy the alien! You've got to eat it **quickly**.
Jimmy: Okay, Mom! I'll save you all!

Jimmy eats the grapes. Suddenly, he says:

Jimmy: There's a big problem.
Julia: What is it, sweetheart?
Jimmy: The tree can't **live** in my belly. It needs **rain**.

Julia smiles and picks up the cauliflower.

Julia: Look, these are **clouds**. If you eat them, the tree will **drink** the rainwater.
Jimmy: Oh, that's perfect! I'll save the tree.

For the first time, Jimmy eats his entire plate. Julia is overjoyed.

From that day on, she **tells him stories** at every meal, and Jimmy always finishes his food.

English	French	Pronunciation
A vegetable	Un légume	[uhn lay-GOOM]
Upset	Fâché	[fa-SHAY]
A meal	Un repas	[uhn ruh-PAH]
A candy (sweets)	Un bonbon	[uhn bon-BON]
Spinach	Les épinards	[lay zay-pee-NAR]
Health	La santé	[la sahn-TAY]
A banana	Une banane	[ewn ba-NAN]
Disgusting	Dégoûtant	[day-goo-TAHN]
A watermelon	Une pastèque	[ewn pas-TEK]
Juicy	Juteux (se)	[zhoo-TUH (zhoo-TUHZ)]
A strawberry	Une fraise	[ewn FREZ]
Sweet	Sucré(e)	[soo-KRAY (soo-KRAY)]
To lie	Mentir	[mahn-TEER]
Real	Vrai(e)	[vray]
To start to	Se mettre à	[suh MET-ruh ah]
Exhausted/Tired	Fatigué(e)	[fa-tee-GAY]
To take care of	S'occuper de	[soh-kew-PAY duh]
Worse	Pire	[peer]
A cauliflower	Un chou-fleur	[uhn shoo-FLUHR]
Grapes	Le raisin	[luh ray-ZAN]
The head	La tête	[la TET]
To destroy	Détruire	[day-TRWEER]
A tree	Un arbre	[uhn AR-bruh]
To save	Sauver	[soh-VAY]
How	Comment	[koh-MAHN]
To hide	Cacher	[ka-SHAY]
In your belly	Dans ton ventre	[dahn ton VAHN-truh]
Quick / Quickly	Vite	[veet]
To live	Vivre	[VEE-vruh]
To drink	Boire	[bwar]
The rain	La pluie	[la PLWEE]
A cloud	Un nuage	[uhn new-AHZH]
From that day on	Depuis ce jour	[duh-PWEE suh ZHOOR]
To tell a story	Raconter une histoire	[ra-kohn-TAY ewn ees-TWAHR]

A. **Sometimes parents need to be quite creative to make their kids eat their veggies! Let's find out what happened here using your understanding of the story. Remember, you're supposed to answer these questions in French.**
   1. How many heads does the alien have?
   2. What does the tree in Jimmy's belly need?

B. **Can you connect the real food elements with their storytelling counterparts?**
   1. Le brocoli   A. un alien
   2. Le raisin   B. un nuage
   3. Le chou-fleur   C. un arbre

C. **Fill in the blanks to complete the story:**
   1. Jimmy veut seulement manger des _____ à chaque repas.
   2. Julia propose à Jimmy une _____ lorsqu'il refuse de manger les épinards.
   3. Julia dit à Jimmy que le brocoli est en fait un _____ magique.
   4. Jimmy dit que l'arbre a besoin de _____ pour vivre.
   5. Après avoir mangé le brocoli et les raisins, Julia prend le _____ et dit que ce sont des nuages.

STORY #8 L'ANNIVERSAIRE

Samuel est un gentil garçon qui aime beaucoup sa famille. Et surtout, il adore offrir des **cadeaux**.

Aujourd'hui, Samuel est **nerveux**. **Samedi**, c'est **l'anniversaire** de son **grand-père**, et il veut lui **acheter** une **montre**. Malheureusement, il n'a pas assez d'**argent**.

Il compte ses **pièces**. Un, deux, trois... Quinze euros ! Il est déçu. Ce n'est pas beaucoup.

Même s'il ne peut pas acheter la montre, il veut tout de même offrir quelque chose à son **papi**.

Alors, il sort de chez lui et marche dans la rue pour aller au magasin à côté de chez lui. À l'intérieur, il y a beaucoup de vêtements d'occasion. Il regarde dans les **cartons** et trouve **un chapeau** marron. Il n'est pas **tout neuf**, mais peut-être que son grand-père l'aimera.

Finalement, il le prend et demande timidement à la **caissière** :

> "Bonjour, madame, **combien** coûte ce chapeau ?"
> "Ah, mais ce chapeau est pour **les grands**, ça ne te va pas !" répond la femme.
> "Je sais, mais ce n'est pas pour moi, c'est un cadeau d'anniversaire pour mon grand-père," dit l'enfant.
> "Oh ! Tu es vraiment un gentil garçon. Normalement, il coûte 20 euros, mais pour ton grand **cœur,** je te le laisse à 15 euros !" s'exclame-t-elle.
> "Oh, merci beaucoup !" dit le petit.

Il prend le chapeau, **donne** l'argent à la vendeuse, et retourne chez lui.

Samedi, toute la famille est réunie pour fêter l'anniversaire. Il y a sa mère, son père, sa sœur Angèle, et même son oncle Charlie, qui est en vacances. Samuel regarde nerveusement son grand-père ouvrir ses cadeaux. Tout le monde a offert des cadeaux beaucoup plus **chers**. L'oncle Charlie a acheté une belle bouteille de **vin**. Samuel n'aime pas le vin, mais il sait que ça coûte cher. Sa sœur Angèle lui a acheté une belle montre. Samuel est un peu jaloux, mais il ne dit **rien** pour ne pas **gâcher** la fête.

Au bout d'un moment, le grand-père ouvre le cadeau de Samuel et, tout d'un coup, **le vieil homme** se met à pleurer.

> "Qui a acheté ce merveilleux chapeau ?" s'exclame-t-il.
> "C'est moi, papi," répond Samuel.
> Son grand-père **le prend dans ses bras** et lui dit : "C'est exactement le même que ta grand-mère m'a acheté **il y a 20 ans** ! Je l'ai perdu et je le regrette tous les jours. C'est **le meilleur** cadeau de la journée !"

Le garçon regarde son grand-père et sourit.

> "**Joyeux anniversaire**, papi !"

Samuel passe toute la fête à **chanter** et à danser. Quel anniversaire **inoubliable** !

Speak Abroad
Academy

STORY #8 THE BIRTHDAY

Samuel is a kind boy who loves his family very much. And above all, he loves giving **gifts**.

Today, Samuel is **nervous**. **Saturday** is his **grandfather's birthday**, and he wants to **buy** him a **watch**. Unfortunately, he doesn't have enough **money**.

He counts his **coins**. One, two, three... Fifteen euros! He's disappointed. It's not much. **Even though** he can't buy the watch, he still wants to get something for his **grandpa**.

So, he leaves his house and walks down the street to the shop next to his home. Inside, there are many **second-hand clothes**. He looks through **the boxes** and finds a brown **hat**. It's not **brand new**, but maybe his grandfather will like it. Finally, he picks it up and timidly asks **the cashier**:

"Hello, ma'am, **how much** is this hat?"
"Oh, but this hat is for **grown ups**, it won't fit you!" the woman replies.
"I know, but it's not for me. It's a birthday gift for my grandpa," says the boy.
"Oh! You're really a sweet boy. Normally, it costs 20 euros, but because you have such a big **heart**, I'll give it to you for 15 euros!" she exclaims.

"Oh, thank you so much!" says the little boy.

He takes the hat, **gives** the money to the cashier, and goes back home.

On Saturday, the whole family is gathered to celebrate the birthday. There's his mother, his father, his sister Angèle, and even his uncle Charlie, who is on vacation. Samuel nervously watches his grandfather open his gifts. Everyone has given much more **expensive** presents. Uncle Charlie bought a nice bottle of **wine**. Samuel doesn't like wine, but he knows it's expensive. His sister Angèle bought him a nice watch. Samuel feels a little jealous, but he says **nothing** so as not **to spoil** the party.

After a while, Grandpa opens Samuel's gift, and suddenly, **the old man** starts to cry.

"Who bought this wonderful hat?" he exclaims.
"It was me, Grandpa," Samuel replies.
His grandfather **hugs** him and says, "It's exactly the same as the one your grandmother bought me 20 **years ago**! I **los**t it and regret it every day. This is **the best** gift of the day!"

The boy looks at his grandfather and smiles.

"**Happy birthday**, Grandpa!"

Samuel spends the rest of the party **singing** and dancing. What an **unforgettable** birthday!

English	French	Pronunciation
A gift / A present	Un cadeau	[uhn kah-DOH]
Nervous	Nerveux (se)	[ner-VUH] / [ner-VUHZ]
A birthday	Un anniversaire	[uhn ah-nee-ver-SAIR]
Grandfather / Grandmother	Grand-père / Grand-mère	[grahn-PAIR] / [grahn-MAIR]
A watch	Une montre	[ewn MON-truh]
Money	Argent	[ar-ZHAHN]
To buy (bought)	Acheter (past. acheté)	[ah-shuh-TAY]
A coin	Une pièce	[ewn PYES]
Saturday	Samedi	[SAHM-dee]
Grandpa	Papi	[PAH-pee]
Something	Quelque chose	[kel-kuh SHOHZ]
Even if/ Even though	Même si	[mem SEE]
Second-hand clothes	Des vêtements d'occasion	[day VET-mahn doh-kah-ZYOHN]
A box	Un carton	[uhn kar-TOHN]
A hat	Un chapeau	[uhn shah-POH]
Brand new	Tout neuf (toute neuve)	[too NUHF] / [toot NUHV]
A cashier	Un caissier / une caissière	[uhn kay-SYAY] / [ewn kay-SYEHR]
How much	Combien	[kohm-BYAN]
Grown ups	Les grands	[lay GRAHN]
A heart	Un cœur	[uhn KUR]
To give (gave)	Donner (past. donné)	[doh-NAY]
Expensive	Cher (chère)	[SHER]
Wine	Le vin	[luh VAHN]
Nothing	Rien	[ryan]
To spoil	Gâcher	[gah-SHAY]
An old man	Un vieil homme	[uhn vyay LOHM]
Wonderful	Merveilleux (se)	[mehr-vay-YEUH] / [mehr-vay-YEUHZ]
To hug	Prendre dans les bras	[prahndr dahn lay BRAH]
___ years ago	Il y a ___ ans	[eel yah ___ AHN]
Lose (lost)	Perdre (past. perdu)	[pairdr] / [pair-DYU]
The best	Le meilleur / la meilleure	[luh MAY-yer] / [lah MAY-yer]

Speak Abroad
Academy

English	French	Pronunciation
Happy birthday !	**Joyeux anniversaire !**	*[zhwa-YEU ah-nee-ver-SAIR]*
To sing	**Chanter**	*[shahn-TAY]*
To dance	**Danser**	*[dahn-SAY]*
Unforgettable	**Inoubliable**	*[ee-noo-blee-AHB-luh]*

A. **Such a touching story. Did you understand it all? Let's find out! Please remember to answer all the questions in French.**

1. What does Samuel want to buy for his grandfather's birthday?
2. How much money does Samuel have when he counts his coins?
3. What does Samuel find in the second-hand shop that he decides to buy?
4. Why does Samuel get jealous of his sister?
5. What does Samuel do after his grandfather reacts to the hat?

B. **Let's see if you can guess the missing words using your understanding of the story!**

1. Samuel est un garçon gentil qui aime beaucoup sa _____ et adore surtout faire des _____.
2. Samuel compte son _____ et trouve qu'il a quinze euros.
3. Il regarde dans les _____ et trouve un _____ marron.
4. L'oncle Charlie a acheté _____ pour l'anniversaire.
5. Le _____ de Samuel dit que le chapeau est exactement le même que celui que sa _____ lui a acheté il y a 20 ans.

STORY # 9 L'ÉCHARPE ROUGE D'EMILY

Aujourd'hui, c'est le jour du Brevet, l'examen final du **collège**. Emily **vérifie** son **cartable**. Elle prend sa **trousse**, un **cahier** et tous ses **stylos**. C'est bon, elle est prête ! **Dehors**, il fait très froid. Alors, elle prend son **manteau** et ses **gants**. Elle veut aussi prendre son écharpe, mais... elle ne la trouve pas.

> "Oh non, mon écharpe **porte-bonheur** ! Je ne peux pas **aller à l'école sans** elle !"

Elle court dans sa chambre et regarde partout. Elle cherche dans son **bureau**, dans son **armoire**, sous le **lit**, sur les étagères. Elle trouve quelques **livres**, mais pas son écharpe.

Elle va dans la cuisine **où** sa mère prépare le petit déjeuner.

Odile :   Emily, pourquoi tu cours partout dans la maison ?
Emily :   Maman, je ne trouve pas mon écharpe rouge !
Odile :   **Ce n'est pas grave**, ma chérie. Je peux te donner **la mienne**, si tu veux.
Emily :   Non, **tu ne comprends pas**. C'est mon écharpe porte-bonheur ! J'ai toujours 20/20 quand j'ai mon écharpe rouge à un examen.
Odile :   C'est ridicule, Emily !
Emily :   Mais c'est vrai, maman ! **J'en ai besoin, sinon** je ne vais pas à l'école.
Odile :   D'accord, ma chérie. Mais elle n'est pas dans la cuisine. Va voir au salon.

Dans le salon, son père est assis sur **le canapé**. **Il regarde la télé**.

Olivier :   Je peux t'aider, Emily ? **Tu as l'air** toute triste.
Emily :   Je cherche mon écharpe rouge. Je ne peux pas aller à mon examen sans elle.
Olivier :   Mais pourquoi ?
Emily :   C'est mon porte-bonheur, tu ne peux pas comprendre.
Olivier :   En tout cas, je suis au salon depuis ce matin. Elle n'est pas ici.

Emily va voir son frère dans sa chambre à l'étage. Il joue à un jeu vidéo sur son **ordinateur**.

Thomas :   Pourquoi tu me **déranges** ? Je suis **occupé**.
Emily :   Désolée, mais je cherche mon écharpe rouge.
Thomas :   "Elle n'est pas dans ma chambre !"

La jeune fille est très triste. Elle a **mal au ventre**. Elle va devoir passer son examen sans son écharpe. Soudain, elle voit son chien dans les escaliers. Il dort confortablement dans **son panier**... et sur son écharpe ! Quand **elle s'approche** de lui, il ouvre les yeux, la regarde et se met à **grogner**. Elle essaie de prendre l'écharpe, mais le chien attrape **l'autre bout** entre ses dents. Tout d'un coup, l'écharpe **se déchire** en deux. Le chien est tout content et **aboie**. Emily est en colère, mais elle n'a plus de choix. Elle va devoir **porter** son écharpe déchirée.

Mais quand elle sort, elle rit joyeusement.

> "**J'espère** que c'est le bout **chanceux** !"

STORY # 9 EMILY'S RED SCARF

Today is the day of the Brevet, the final exam of **middle school**. Emily **checks** her **schoolbag**. She grabs her **pencil case**, a **notebook**, and all her **pens**. She's ready! **Outside**, it's very cold. So, she puts on her **coat** and **gloves**. She also wants to take her **scarf**, but... she can't find it.

"Oh no, my **lucky** scarf! I can't **go to school without** it!"

She runs to her room and looks everywhere. She searches through her **desk**, in her **wardrobe**, under the **bed**, on the **shelves**. She finds a few **books** but not her scarf.

She goes to the kitchen, **where** her mother is preparing breakfast.

Odile:	Emily, why are you running all over the house?
Emily:	Mom, I can't find my red scarf!
Odile:	**It's not a big deal**, sweetheart. I can give you **mine** if you want.
Emily:	No, **you don't understand**. It's my lucky scarf! I always get 20/20 when I wear my red scarf to an exam.
Odile:	That's ridiculous, Emily!
Emily:	But it's true, Mom! **I need it, otherwise**, I'm not going to school.
Odile:	Alright, sweetheart. But it's not in the kitchen. Go check the living room.

In the living room, her father is sitting on **the couch**. **He's watching TV**.

Olivier:	Can I help you, Emily? **You look** so sad.
Emily:	I'm looking for my red scarf. I can't go to my exam without it.
Olivier:	But why?
Emily:	It's my lucky charm, you wouldn't understand.
Olivier:	Anyway, I've been in the living room all morning. It's not here.

Emily goes to see her brother in his room **upstairs**. He's playing **a video game** on his **computer**.

Thomas:	Why are you **bothering** me? **I'm busy**.
Emily:	Sorry, but I'm looking for my red scarf.
Thomas:	It's not in my room!

The young girl is very upset. **Her stomach hurts**. She's going to have to take her exam without her scarf. Suddenly, she sees her dog on the stairs. He's sleeping comfortably in his **basket**... on top of her scarf! When she **gets closer**, he opens his eyes, looks at her, and starts **growling**. She tries to grab the scarf, but the dog bites down on **the other end**. All of a sudden, the scarf **tears** in two. The dog is very happy and **barks**. Emily is angry, but she has no other choice. She'll have to **wear** her torn scarf.

But as she leaves, she laughs cheerfully.

"I **hope** this is the lucky **half**!"

English	French	Pronunciation
Middle school	**Le collège**	*[luh koh-LEZH]*
To check	**Vérifier**	*[veh-REE-fee-ay]*
A school bag	**Un cartable**	*[uh kar-TAH-bluh]*
A pencil case	**Une trousse**	*[ewn TROOS]*
A notebook	**Un cahier**	*[uhn KAH-yay]*
A pen	**Un stylo**	*[uhn STEE-loh]*
Outside	**Dehors**	*[duh-OHR]*
A coat	**Un manteau**	*[uhn MAHN-toh]*
A glove	**Un gant**	*[uhn GAHN]*
A scarf	**Une écharpe**	*[ewn ay-SHAR-puh]*
A lucky charm (lucky)	**Un porte-bonheur**	*[uhn port boh-NEUR]*
To go to (school)	**Aller à (l'école)**	*[ah-LAY ah lay-KOHL]*
With / Without	**Avec / Sans**	*[ah-VEK / SAHN]*
A desk	**Un bureau**	*[uhn bew-ROH]*
A wardrobe	**Une armoire**	*[ewn ar-MWAHR]*
A bed	**Un lit**	*[uhn LEE]*
A shelf	**Un étagère**	*[ewn ay-tah-ZHAIR]*
A book	**Un livre**	*[uhn LEEV-ruh]*
Where	**Où**	*[OO]*
It's not a big deal	**Ce n'est pas grave**	*[suh nay pah GRAHV]*
Mine	**Le mien / la mienne**	*[luh MYEHN / lah MYEHN]*
To understand	**Comprendre**	*[kohm-PRAHN-druh]*
I need it	**J'en ai besoin**	*[zhahn nay buh-ZWEN]*
Otherwise	**Sinon**	*[see-NOHN]*
To watch TV	**Regarder la télé**	*[ruh-gahr-DAY lah TAY-lay]*
A couch	**Un canapé**	*[uhn kah-nah-PAY]*
You look / You seem	**Tu as l'air**	*[tew ah LAYR]*
Upstairs	**À l'étage**	*[ah lay-TAHZH]*
A video game	**Un jeu vidéo**	*[uhn zhuh vee-DAY-oh]*
A computer	**Un ordinateur**	*[uhn or-dee-nah-TEUR]*

Speak Abroad
Academy

English	French	Pronunciation
To bother / to disturb	**Déranger**	[day-RAHN-zhay]
I'm busy	**Je suis occupé(e)**	[zhuh swee zo-koo-PAY]
A stomachache (hurt)	**Un mal au ventre**	[uhn mahl oh VAHN-truh]
A (wicker) basket	**Un panier**	[uhn pan-YAY]
To get closer	**S'approcher**	[sah-pro-SHAY]
To growl	**Grogner**	[groh-NYAY]
To catch	**Attraper**	[ah-trah-PAY]
A tooth / teeth	**Une dent / des dents**	[ewn DAHN / day DAHN]
One end/ the other end	**Un bout/ l'autre bout**	[uhn BOO / lohtr BOO]
To tear	**Déchirer**	[day-shee-RAY]
To bark	**Aboyer**	[ah-bwah-YAY]
To wear	**Porter**	[por-TAY]
To hope	**Espérer**	[ess-pay-RAY]
Lucky	**Chanceux (se)**	[shahn-SUH / shahn-SUHZ]

A. **Careful what you wish for! Emily did eventually find her scarf but was she that lucky? Let's see if you understood the text by answering these questions in French.**
1. Why is Emily looking everywhere in her bedroom ?
2. What is Emily's father doing in the living room?
3. Who is playing a video game on his computer?

B. **Where is everyone? Can you connect each member of the family to their location?**
1. Thomas   A. le salon
2. Odile   B. le panier
3. Olivier   C. la chambre
4. Le chien   D. la cuisine

C. **These sentences are all wrong according to the story. Let's see if you can correct them by replacing one word in each sentence.**
1. Emily cherche son manteau rouge porte-bonheur.
2. La maman d'Emily prépare le dîner dans la cuisine.
3. Le chien d'Emily joue dans son panier.

CONCLUSION

As we close the final chapter of this journey through the French language, it's time to pause and reflect on some of the fundamental concepts we have covered. From the foundational stones of grammar to the vibrant threads of daily conversations and the vivid narratives of short stories, this book has been a guide, a companion, and a portal into the heart of French culture.

In Section I, we embarked on an exploration of French grammar. We started with the basics; pronouns and greetings; the keys to building new connections. Then, we navigated nouns and articles, learning to name the world around us. Our journey through describing people, places, and things painted our conversations with the colors of life, while more descriptors added depth and texture. We covered possessives, demonstratives and celebrated the pleasures of eating and drinking, expressed our likes and dislikes, and mastered the art of negation.

Moreover, asking questions opened doors to understanding, and discussions of time, dates, and seasons rooted our conversations in the rhythm of life. With more essentials, possessives, and reflexives, we delved deeper into the essence of communication and self-expression.

Section II transitioned us from the structured world of grammar to words and phrases. Everyday essentials, shopping & dining out and travel & transportation prepared us for adventures while health needs & emergencies ensured we were never lost in translation, even in the most critical moments. Section III was where we lived the language through short stories that further immersed you in the cultural and emotional nuances of French life.

This book isn't just about learning French; it is about living it. With every new term, phrase, and story, you don't just memorize; you internalize. You don't just study; you experience. And as you part ways with this book, remember that your journey with French doesn't end here. It continues in every conversation you engage in, every book you read, and every dream you dream in the language of *Molière*.

So here's to you, dear learner, for embarking on this journey with us. May the knowledge you've gained be the wings that lift you into new horizons, the key that unlocks more doors, and the light that guides you through the enchanting world of French language and culture. *Bon voyage et bonne chance!*

ANSWER KEY

CHAPTER 1
1.1 Pronouns

A	1. Nous	2. Je	3. Elles	4. Ils	5. Tu
	6. Vous	7. Nous	8. Ils		
B	1. Je	2. Nous	3. Vous	4. Ils	5. Tu
C	1. Ils	2. Vous	3. Vous	4. Nous	5. Il
D	1. Tu	2. Tu	3. Vous	4. Vous	5. Tu
	6. Vous	7. Vous	8. Tu	9. Tu	10. Vous
E	1. Tu	2. Vous	3. Vous	4. Vous	5. Vous

1.3 Language Etiquette

A	1. B	2. C	3. D	4. E	5. A
B	1. Salut/Bonjour	2. Bonjour	3. Salut/Bonjour	4. Salut/Bonsoir	5. Bonjour
C	1. A	2. C	3. D	4. B	5. E
D	1. E	2. C	3. D	4. A	5. B
E	1. ça va ?	2. et toi ?	3. bien	4. À	5. Au revoir

CHAPTER 2
2.1 Gender of Nouns

1. La (photo)	2. L' (hospital)	3. La (television)	4. Le (program)	5. Le (system)
6. Le (problem)	7. La (planet)	8. L' (hotel)	9. La (person)	10. L' (animal)
11. La (conversation)	12. Le (telephone)			

2.2 Plural Nouns

A	1. Les hommes	2. Les amies	3. Les conversations	4. Les animaux	5. Les systèmes
	6. Les chats	7. Les maisons	8. Les trains	9. Les villes	10. Les médecins
B	1. Le chien	2. La télévision	3. La femme	4. La chienne	5. L'hôpital
	6. La fille	7. Le garçon	8. La salade	9. Le bâtiment	10. La voiture

2.3 Indefinite Article

A	1. Des grands-pères		2. Des livres		3. Des chiens		4. Des femmes		5. Des étudiants	
	6. Des médecins		7. Des hôtels		8. Des trains		9. Des chats		10. Des villes	
B	1. Les étudiants		2. Les planètes		3. Un médecin		4. Des photos		5. La femme	
	6. Les soeurs		7. Des amis		8. Un chien		9. La mère		10. Des maisons	
C	1. La		2. des		3. la		4. une		5. des	
	6. le		7. un		8. les		9. la		10. une	
D	1. The woman		2. The house		3. The chicken		4. The boy		5. The brothers	
	6. The doctor		7. The train		8. The planets		9. A cat		10. Some dogs	
	11. The phone		12. The drinks		13. A program		14. Some systems		15. The books	
E	1. La	2. des	3. une	4. Le	5. une	6. les	7. le	8. un	9. les	10. les
F	1. une		2. une		3. la		4. La		5. Le	

CHAPTER 3
3.1 Singular Adjectives

A	1. grande	2. pauvre	3. fidèle	4. jolie	5. difficile
	6. bon	7. vieux	8. intéressant	9. forte	10. petite
B	1. pauvre	2. bonne	3. petite	4. gentil	5. vieux
	6. mauvais	7. intelligente	8. loyale	9. fort	10. grosse
C	1. Difficile	2. Grand	3. Bon	4. gentille	5. Faible

3.2 Plural Adjectives

A	1. Les grandes tomates	2. Les petits hommes	3. Les chiens intelligents	4. Les filles fortes	5. Les personnes gentilles
	6. Les petites villes	7. Les chats minces	8. Les femmes heureuses	9. Les livres difficiles	10. Les excellentes nourritures
B	1. intéressants	2. travailleuse	3. belle	4. petits	5. jolis
	6. bonnes	7. gros	8. gentils		

3.3 Nationality

1. américaine	2. française	3. anglaise	4. italienne	5. espagnol

3.4 Describing a Person

A	1. jeune	2. petit	3. intéressant	4. drôle	5. loyal
B	1. intelligente	2. gros	3. belle	4. gentille	5. vieux
C	1. Marc est français.	2. Le garçon est grand.	3. La fille est intelligente.	4. L'homme est gentil.	5. La femme est belle/jolie.
D	1. français	2. américaine	3. anglais	4. italien	5. française

CHAPTER 4
4.1 Adjectives

A	1. nouvelle	2. joyeuse	3. gros	4. méchant	5. vieux
	6. chère	7. grand	8. lente	9. bruyant	10. long
B	1. jaune	2. bleue	3. orange	4. blanche	5. noire
	6. gris	7. vert	8. rose	9. marron	10. rouge
C	1. lent – rapide	2. noir – blanche	3. grande – petit	4. gros – mince	5. vieux – jeune
D	1. grand et vieux	2. laide et pauvre	3. vieille et petite	4. joyeux et rapide	5. facile

4.2 Demonstrative Adjectives

A	1. Ce manteau est beau	2. Ces chaussures sont chères	3. Cette chemise est douce	4. Ces bottes sont élégantes	5. Ce chapeau est propre
B	1. Cette	2. Ce	3. Cette	4. Ces	5. Cet

4.3 Describing Nouns

A	1. Cette	2. Ce – cet	3. Cette – ces	4. Cette	
B	1. sont	2. est – sont	3. est	4. sont – est	5. est
	6. sont – sont	7. sont	8. est	9. sont	10. sont – est

Answer key

CHAPTER 5

A	1. Thomas et Adeline	2. Thomas et Adeline	3. Paul	4. Parce qu'ils sont des touristes et New York est une grande ville	5. Une carte
B	1. est italien	2. est mexicaine	3. est américain	4. est allemand	5. est française
	6. est espagnol	7. est portugais	8. est anglais	9. est autrichien	10. est américaine
C	1. sommes	2. es	3. sont	4. suis – es	5. est
	6. sont	7. sont	8. sommes	9. est	10. est
	11. êtes	12. êtes	13. suis	14. est	15. est – est
	16. sont	17. êtes	18. sont	19. es	20. suis
D	1. Nous sommes	2. Ils sont	3. Je suis	4. Tu es	5. Vous êtes
	6. Nous sommes	7. Elles sont	8. Ils sont	9. Tu es	10. Vous êtes
E	1. Anna est au musée.	2. Nous sommes dehors.	3. Elsa et Jane sont à l'école.	4. Ils sont à la banque.	5. Il est au supermarché.
	6. Nous sommes dans la voiture.	7. Tu es heureux.	8. Je suis jeune et beau.	9. Vous êtes très intelligent.	10. Vous êtes au supermarché.
F	1. sommes – la voiture	2. est – est – la maison	3. suis – est	4. est – Elle est française	5. es – suis

CHAPTER 6
6.1 Present Tense Avoir

A	1. Nous avons	2. J'ai	3. Tu as	4. J'ai	5. Elle a
	6. Ils ont	7. Il a	8. Elles ont	9. Vous avez	10. Nous avons
B	1. Je suis	2. Vous avez	3. Il a – Il est	4. Elle a – elle est	5. Ils ont
	6. Nous sommes	7. J'ai	8. Tu es – tu as	9. Elles sont – elles sont	10. Nous avons
C	1. J'ai	2. Ils ont – ils ont	3. Elle a – il a	4. Vous avez	5. Elles ont
	6. Nous avons	7. J'ai	8. Tu as		
D	1. Trois	2. Zéro	3. Paul	4. Paul. Cinq	5. Francine

6.2 Age

A	1. J'ai vingt-cinq ans.	2. J'ai trente ans.	3. J'ai trente-sept ans.	4. J'ai quarante-et-un ans.	5. J'ai quatre-vingt-dix ans.
B	1. Elle a vingt ans.	2. Nous avons quinze ans.	3. Ils ont quatre-vingt-cinq ans.	4. Elles ont quatre-vingt-six ans.	5. Tu as vingt-neuf ans.
	6. Vous avez soixante ans.	7. J'ai trente-huit ans.	8. Il a cent ans.		
C	1. Elle est jeune.	2. Il est vieux.	3. Nous sommes jeunes.	4. Nous sommes vieux/vieilles.	5. Ils sont vieux.
	6. Je suis jeune.	7. Tu es jeune.	8. Elles sont vieilles.	9. Elle est jeune.	10. Il est vieux.

6.3 Quantity

A	1. Marie has ten cats. She has too many cats!	2. I have more children than Jennifer.	3. He has a lot of uncles and aunts. They are too noisy.	4. They have a little money.	5. We have too many problems.
	6. Nina has less friends than Natasha.	7. James has ten dollars. Jim has fifteen dollars. Jim has more money than James.	8. Daniel and Emily have thirty dollars. We have less money than Daniel and Emily.		

B	1. a moins de chats que Bob.	2. a plus de filles que Charlie.	3. a moins d'argent que Daniel.	4. a plus de livres qu'Emily.	5. J'ai plus de voitures que George.
C	1. Six	2. Neuf	3. Isabelle	4. Isabelle	5. Deux cents

CHAPTER 7
7.1 Demonstratives

A	1. Il y a une fleur dans le jardin.	2. Il y a un ordinateur sur la table.	3. Il y a une femme devant la voiture.	4. Il y a un chat derrière la maison.	5. Il y a une fille sous la table.
B	1. Il y a des femmes dans le jardin.	2.Il y a des clés sur la table.	3. Il y a trois chats sous la voiture.	4. Il y a un grand homme dehors.	5. Il y a des fleurs rouges et jaunes dans le jardin.

7.2 Household Vocabulary

A	1. The walls are white.	2. The house is small, but the garden is big.	3. I like the kitchen. It's beautiful and new.	4. She's in the living room.	5. We are in the office.
	6. The family is in the dining room.	7. The black car is in the garage. The red car is outside.	8. The woman is in the bathroom.		
B	1. I am a driver. I have three cars in the garage. One is black. Two are red.	2. Caroline is a friendly girl. She has thirty friends and they are friendly too.	3. There's a tall man in the garage. It's my father. And the friendly woman in the kitchen? That's my mother.	4. The woman in the restaurant is old. She's eighty-six years old and she has eight daughters.	5. These blue shoes are new. And these green shoes are new too. I have too many shoes.

7.3 Aller

A	1. Tu vas	2. Il va	3. Elles vont	4. Je vais	5. Vous allez
	6. Elle va	7. Ils vont	8. Nous allons	9. Vous allez	10. Je vais
B	1. It's a beautiful day. We are going to the park.	2. The supermarket is behind the bakery.	3. I'm in the garden and you're going to work.	4. The woman in the car is going to the bank.	5. Emily and Daniel are going to the museum with their friends.
	6. My mother is at home. My father is going to the supermarket.	7. The family is going to the restaurant.	8. He's going to the bar in his new car.	9. There's a dog in front of the restaurant.	10. I'm going to the house! There's a cow outside.

7.4 Correct Sentences

A	1. X	2. ✓	3. X	4. X	5. ✓	6. X	7. ✓	8. ✓	9. ✓	10. X
B	1. Je vais bien.		2. C'est un beau chien/ Ce sont des beaux chiens.		3. J'aime ces femmes, elles sont belles.		4. Nous avons/ Vous avez un examen.		5. Il est médecin.	
C	1. va		2. est		3. ont		4. avez		5. allons	

CHAPTER 8
8.1 Faire

A	1. Tu fais	2. Je fais	3. Nous faisons	4. Ils font	5. Il fait
	6. Elles font	7. Elle fait	8. Vous faites		
B	1. We are making a cake in the kitchen.	2. The tall woman is exercising in the garden.	3. The two friends are doing sports in the park.	4. The kind man is doing the dishes.	5. Emily and Erica are at the shops. They are shopping.

8.2 Weather

A	1. Il pleut	2. Il fait froid	3. Il fait chaud	4. Il pleut	5. Il fait chaud
B	1. A	2. A	3. A		

8.3 Vouloir

1. Tu veux	2. Je veux	3. Elle veut	4. Nous voulons	5. Ils veulent

8.4 Conditional Vouloir

A	1. Il voudrait des fleurs.	2. Nous voudrions trois cafés, s'il vous plaît.	3. Je voudrais une chemise bleue et une jupe blanche.	4. Ils voudraient une table	5. Elle voudrait un manteau noir.
B	1. The grandmother.	2. A new cat.	3. Next to the bakery.	4. 4 cats	5. Anna
C	1. We're shopping at the supermarket. Fruits are expensive!	2. The weather is good. There are flowers in the park. I want to go to the park.	3. He's making the bed. You're doing the dishes. And me? I'm at a bar with friends.	4. It's raining. The new clothes are wet.	5. It's cold today! I would like a hot coffee. She wants coffee too.

8.5 Porter

A	1. Il porte	2. Tu portes	3. Elles portent	4. Elle porte	5. Je porte
B	1. It's a beautiful day. I'm wearing a new shirt and we're going to an expensive restaurant.	2. I'm wearing a brown jacket, but I would like a black jacket.	3. It's hot today. I'm wearing sunglasses and shorts. I'm going to the park with friends.	4. She wears expensive clothes, but these clothes are old and ugly.	5. I would like four small yellow hats, please. They are for my cats!

CHAPTER 9
9.1 Food

A	1. Bread and cheese	2. Fish and vegetables	3. Coffee with sugar	4. Chicken and beef	5. Tea with milk
B	1. Ten eggs	2. Five apples	3. Fifteen potatoes	4. Three bananas	5. Thirty-five lemons
C	1. Je voudrais un café avec du lait et du sucre.	2. Nous voudrions de la viande et des légumes.	3. Il voudrait une bière et elle voudrait un jus.	4. Elle voudrait des champignons dans la salade.	5. Ils voudraient du pain et du beurre.
D	1. She would like ice cream on top of the cake.	2. He would like fish and vegetables for dinner.	3. I would like a beer with dinner.	4. I would like strawberries and chocolate.	5. They would like eggs, ham, and bread.

9.2 Units of Food

A	1. A spoonful of sugar	2. A cup of milk	3. A handful of strawberries	4. A plate of sausages	5. A bottle of wine
B	1. There's a cup of coffee on the table.	2. There's a plate of eggs and ham in the kitchen.	3. There's tea in the cup, but I would like a coffee.	4. There are five bottles of beer on the table in the garden.	5. There's a bottle of wine in the bedroom. It's for Marie's birthday.

9.3 Manger

A	1. Elles mangent	2. Tu manges	3. Je mange	4. Ils mangent	5. Elle mange
B	1. Je mange une pomme au petit-déjeuner.	2. Nous mangeons une grande assiette de poisson. C'est délicieux !	3. Ils mangent dans le jardin ce soir.	4. Elle mange une poignée de fraises.	5. Il mange de la glace pour le dessert.

9.4 Boire

A	1. Every night, he drinks too much beer and I eat too much cake.	2. We are at the restaurant. There's a big plate of beef on the table. It's delicious!	3. For breakfast, I drink coffee with sugar and milk. Louis drinks a glass of apple juice.	4. There's a plate of eggs and sausages in the kitchen. It's for you!	5. Andy and Angela drink a lot of wine. Bob and I, we eat a lot of salad.
B	1. Un restaurant français populaire	2. Huit	3. Ils travaillent ensemble	4. Quatre bouteilles de vin	5. De la viande de boeuf, du poulet, du poisson et des légumes

CHAPTER 10
10.1 Aimer

1. aimes	2. aime	3. aimons	4. aimez	5. aime
6. aime	7. aiment	8. aiment		

10.2 Hobbies

1. Nous aimons beaucoup la musique.	2. J'aime les romans de fiction.	3. Ils aiment la photographie.	4. Il aime les jeux de société.	5. Tu aimes beaucoup l'art.

10.3 Faire + Hobbies

A	1. Il aime jouer aux échecs.	2. Elle aime faire de la pâtisserie	3. Ils aiment jouer aux jeux vidéo.	4. J'aime jouer aux jeux de société.	5. Tu aimes écouter de la musique et j'aime danser.
B	1. They like to play together in the garden.	2. She likes to do sports at school.	3. We like to listen to music in the morning.	4. He likes to eat cakes. I like to make cakes.	5. I like to watch television with my friend.
	6. They like to go shopping in Paris.	7. You like to do gardening.	8. You like to read interesting books.		
C	1. He has a television because he likes movies.	2. Rachel likes meat. She would like a plate of chicken, please.	3. I like to play soccer with the white dog	4. We like to play video games with beautiful women.	5. They like flowers. Every day, they like to garden together.

10.4. Dislikes

A	1. Tu n'aimes pas	2. Je n'aime pas	3. Nous n'aimons pas	4. Elle n'aime pas	5. Ils n'aiment pas
B	1. Je n'aime pas les musées.	2. Elle n'aime pas les chats noirs.	3. Nous n'aimons pas le vin.	4. Ils n'aiment pas manger dans des restaurants chers.	5. Vous n'aimez pas regarder la télévision.
	6. Ils n'aiment pas manger de la glace.	7. Vous n'aimez pas jouer au tennis.	8. Il n'aime pas lire dans le jardin.		
C	1. Ils aiment cuisiner.	2. Il aime porter des chaussures.	3. Elle aime boire de la bière.	4. Ils aiment manger du fromage.	5. Nous aimons regarder la télévision le soir.
D	1. Il veut un grand jardin. Il aime jardiner.	2. Elle mange beaucoup, mais elle n'aime pas les légumes.	3. J'aime la couleur jaune. Je n'aime pas la couleur noire.	4. Nous aimons le pain à la boulangerie. Nous n'aimons pas le pain au restaurant.	5. Ils n'aiment pas regarder la télévision ensemble.

Speak Abroad
Academy

CHAPTER 11

11.1 Ne… pas

A	1. Je ne suis pas une vache.	2. Je ne mange pas de gâteau.	3. Je ne vais pas à la gare.	4. Je n'ai pas de gentil frère.	5. Je ne veux pas de nouveau chat.
	6. Je ne voudrais pas de bol de cerises.	7. Je ne porte pas de chapeau bleu.	8. Je n'aime pas les fleurs.	9. Je ne bois pas de verre de vin.	10. Je n'ai pas quarante ans.
B	1. Vous n'aimez pas le parapluie jaune.	2. Il ne veut pas de verre d'eau.	3. Elle ne va pas manger sortir.	4. Elles ne portent pas de nouveaux vêtements.	5. Nous ne buvons pas beaucoup de jus d'orange.
	6. Ils ne sont pas des hommes riches.	7. Elle n'est pas triste.	8. Nous n'avons pas deux fils.	9. Vous n'allez pas à l'école.	10. Tu ne travailles pas beaucoup.
C	1. Elle ne veut pas de la petite maison.	2. Je ne veux pas lire un livre.	3. Nous ne mangeons pas de viande.	4. Ils n'ont pas de chat blanc.	5. Je ne suis pas médecin.
D	1. Je mange pas de viande.	2 & 3 CORRECT	4. Nous ne voulons jouer.	5. CORRECT	6. Ils sont pas grands.
E	1. Je ne mange pas de viande.	2. Nous ne voulons pas jouer.	3. Ils ne sont pas grands.		

11.2. Ne… jamais

A	1. Elle n'a jamais d'argent.	2. Le grand homme ne va jamais au supermarché.	3. Je ne mange jamais de viande.	4. Nous n'allons jamais à l'école.	5. Ils ne prennent jamais le petit-déjeuner ensemble.
	6. Vous ne buvez jamais de bière.	7. Elles ne font jamais le lit.	8. Tu ne vas jamais à l'église.		
B	1, 3, 5				
C	1. Il ne travaille jamais.	3. Je ne sors jamais de la maison	5. Vous n'aimez pas cuisiner avec moi.		
D	1. Deux ans	2. Noisy (bruyant)	3. Les légumes	4. Au restaurant	5. Des vacances
E	1. She doesn't like to eat dessert. She eats salads.	2. I have five children; I never go to the movies!	3. He likes to go to expensive restaurants, but he never has any money.	4. You like sad poetry. You are never happy!	5. We never drink beer. We would like to have two glasses of wine.

CHAPTER 12

12.1 Est-ce que

A	1. Est-ce que nous aimons la voiture orange ?	2. Est-ce qu'elle va à la gare ?	3. Est-ce qu'ils sont jeunes ?	4. Est-ce que nous avons une belle voiture ?	5. Est-ce que Jenny a plus d'argent que James ?
B	1. Est-ce que tu aimes les chiens ?	2. Est-ce que c'est un vieil homme ?	3. Est-ce qu'ils vont au restaurant français ?	4. Est-ce que vous êtes riches ?	5. Est-ce qu'ils vont aller à la boulangerie ?

12.2 Inversions

A	1. As-tu une voiture?	2. Boit-il du vin ?	3. Aimez-vous le nouveau restaurant ?	4. Fait-elle du sport ?	5. Aiment-elles jouer au football ?
B	1. Faites-vous toujours du sport les week-ends ?	2. Dois-je finir mon examen ce matin ?	3. Est-elle contente de venir ici ?	4. Va-t-il au bureau le samedi ?	5. Es-tu content de regarder ce film avec moi ?

12.3. Who, What, Where

1. Mon école est devant l'église.	2. C'est mon père.	3. Le violet est ma couleur préférée.	4. Ma femme est écrivaine.	5. Il est à côté du nouveau restaurant.

12.4. When, How, Why

1. Il commence ce soir.	2. Mon mari va très bien.	3. Elle va venir ce soir.	4. Quand nous allons au restaurant français.	5. Mon frère ne va pas bien.

12.5. Pourquoi

1. I have a cat because I like cats.	2. He's outside because he doesn't like the dog.	3. You are wearing shorts because it's hot.	4. We play chess a lot because we're intelligent.	5. You eat five bowls of ice cream because you're sad.

12.6. Expressions + Prepositions

A	1. Who does Jacob go to the restaurant with?	2. She wants a jacket? Which one?	3. Who am I making a cake for?	4. Whose house are you in?	5. Where do they come from?
B	1. Sasha	2. À la boulangerie	3. Une chemise noire et un jean	4. Derrière l'église	5. De Max

CHAPTER 13
13.1 Asking for Time

A	1. Correct	2. X	3. Correct	4. X	
B	1. À quelle heure est le film ?	2. À quelle heure est le concert ?	3. À quelle heure est la fête d'anniversaire?	4. À quelle heure est la classe d'art?	5. À quelle heure est le pique-nique ?
C	1. 1p.m.	2. 8:20 a.m.	3. 11:15 p.m	4. 7:30 a.m.	5. 6:33p.m.
D	1. Dix heures quarante	2. Six heures dix	3. Quinze heures cinq	4. Dix-neuf heures cinquante	5. Vingt-trois heures dix-huit
E	1. Neuf heures	2. Dix heures et demie	3. Midi	4. Une heure et quart	5. Deux heures moins le quart
	6. Quatre heures et demie	7. Huit heures moins le quart	8. Dix heures et quart		

13.2 Expressing Date

A	1. octobre	2. février	3. juin	4. avril	5. août
	6. juillet	7. mercredi	8. vendredi	9. mardi	10. samedi
	11. hier	12. demain	13. aujourd'hui	14. le mois prochain	
B	1. On est jeudi aujourd'hui.	2. Le mois prochain c'est novembre.	3. Il arrive en mars.	4. Le concert est la semaine prochaine.	5. Le samedi, nous allons au parc.
C	1. C'est l'automne	2. C'est l'été.	3. C'est l'hiver.	4. C'est le printemps.	

13.3 Frequency

A	1. Parfois, je mange un bol de fraises.	2. Ils vont souvent au parc.	3. Est-ce l'hiver ? Je veux une tasse de chocolat chaud!	4. C'est le soir ! La fête est à dix-neuf heures.	5. Chaque matin, nous prenons un gros petit-déjeuner ensemble.

Answer key

B	1. Each Sunday, he goes to the bakery and he eats a croissant.	2. Each summer, we go to the beach. It's hot in August!	3. It's April. In Spring, I like to read in the garden.	4. In winter, you wear an elegant black coat. You look beautiful!	5. It's noon and I'm thirsty. Every afternoon, I drink a big glass of water.

CHAPTER 14
14.1 Parler

A	1. Je parle français.	2. Tu parles italien.	3. Vous parlez espagnol.	4. Nous parlons chinois.	5. Elle parle japonais.
	6. Il parle anglais.	7. Ils parlent allemand.	8. Elles parlent portugais.		
B	1. Nous parlons ensemble chaque semaine.	2. Ils parlent à Alex une fois par mois.	3. Elles parlent parfois espagnol.	4. L'homme intelligent parle très bien le français.	5. Chaque matin, tu parles au bébé.
	6. Je ne parle pas espagnol.	7. Elle parle beaucoup.	8. Pourquoi parles-tu à la vache?		
C	1. I like to talk to my grandmother. She's very funny and interesting.	2. I talk to Jane every week because we are good friends.	3. Why do you talk to the cat? The cat doesn't speak English!	4. Who is talking? Is it Emma and Esther? They talk too much.	5. He talks to the dogs because he likes animals.

14.2 Conjunctions

A	1. et	2. ou	3. mais	4. ou	5. mais
B	1. puis	2. comme	3. donc	4. si	5. comme

14.3 Prepositions

A	1. Après	2. jusqu'à	3. sauf	4. avant	5. pendant
B	1. I go to school every day except Sunday.	2. He plays football until noon.	3. You are eating and drinking during an important concert.	4. They go to the museum with an old woman.	5. We don't like to eat before doing sports.
C	1. Nous mangeons le dessert après le dîner.	2. Je fais un gâteau sans sucre.	3. Ils parlent pendant le film.	4. Elle aime lire avant le petit-déjeuner.	5. Il boit du vin avec un homme intéressant.

CHAPTER 15
15.1 Possessive Adjectives

A	1. Son livre	2. Mon chien	3. Notre voiture noire	4. Ton bureau	5. Son verre de vin
B	1. Leur père est mon médecin.	2. Sa veste est rouge et ma veste est blanche.	3. Il ne parle pas à sa mère.	4. Votre fils joue au football avec notre fils.	5. Ma soeur aime manger dans votre restaurant.
C	1. Mes fleurs	2. Ses manteaux	3. Leurs voitures	4. Nos fromages	5. Vos canapés
D	1. Ma sœur n'aime pas ta sœur.	2. Où sont tes frères ?	3. Tes chats sont dans mon jardin.	4. La femme intelligente est leur avocate.	5. Parfois, nos filles vont au parc ensemble.

15.2 Reflexive Pronouns & Verbs

A	1. Je m'	2. Elle se	3. Il se	4. Nous nous	5. Elles se
	6. Tu te	7. Vous vous	8. Ils se		

B	1. À huit heures	2. Un quart d'heure	3. Paul se brosse les dents	4. Il se rase	5. Il s'habille
C	1. Il se déshabille.	2. Je me prépare.	3. Elles se regardent.	4. Ils se rasent.	5. Tu te calmes.
	6. Nous nous réveillons.	7. Elle s'habille.	8. Vous vous reposez.		

15.3 Pouvoir

A	1. Tu peux	2. Je peux	3. Elles peuvent	4. Ils peuvent	5. Vous pouvez
	6. Nous pouvons	7. Elle peut	8. Il peut		
B	1. Je ne peux pas aller au musée.	2. Tu ne peux pas manger de fromage.	3. Elle ne peut pas prendre le croissant.	4. Il ne peut pas parler à la vache.	5. Vous ne pouvez pas préparer le petit-déjeuner.
	6. Nous ne pouvons pas manger dans le jardin.	7. Ils ne peuvent pas parler français.	8. Ils ne peuvent pas porter de chaussettes à la plage.		
C	1. C'est dimanche aujourd'hui. Il y a deux hommes devant ma maison. Ce sont mes amis. Nous allons au musée ensemble.	2. À 17 heures, je me prépare pour la fête. Je porte une belle robe noire et des chaussures blanches.	3. Pour le dessert ce soir, nous avons du gâteau. Veux-tu de la glace sur le gâteau ?	4. Mon frère aime la poésie et ma sœur le tennis. Et moi ? J'aime notre chat.	5. Au printemps, ils vont au parc. En été, ils vont à la plage. Il fait trop chaud, alors je vais à l'église.

SHORT STORIES
STORY #1: La Nouvelle Maison

A	1. The armchair in the living room is very old. Le fauteuil du salon est très vieux.	2. The fridge is next to the oven. Le frigo est contre le four.	3. Samuel can have a dog. Samuel peut avoir un chien.	4. In the garden, there is a swing, some trees, and flowers. Dans le jardin, il y a une balançoire, des arbres et des fleurs.	5. Samuel can store his toys in his new room. Samuel peut ranger ses jouets dans sa nouvelles chambre.
B	1. ses amis	2. trop petite	3. dans le jardin	4. une baignoire	5. dormir sans sa sœur

STORY #2: Le Malentendu

A	1. Peter est ingénieur. (Peter is an engineer.)	2. Devant son ordinateur. (In front of this computer.)	3. Il regarde une vidéo amusante. (He's watching a funny video.)	4. Il lit un journal. (He's reading a newspaper.)
B	1. Peter est un jeune ingénieur. Il travaille tous les jours devant son ordinateur.		2. Peter est en colère parce que l'inconnu mange ses frites. Mais c'est une erreur parce qu'il y a deux assiettes de frites sur la table.	
C	1. L'histoire se passe un mercredi.	2. Peter aime regarder des vidéos amusantes.	3. L'inconnu est assis à droite de Peter.	4. L'inconnu a mangé les 5 dernières frites.

STORY #3: L'animal de compagnie

A	1. François veut adopter un gros chien pour garder leur maison. (François wants to adopt a big dog to guard their house.)	2. Céline préfère un chat parce que les chats sont petits, propres, mignons, et coûtent moins cher à nourrir. (Céline prefers a cat because cats are small, clean, cute, and cost less to feed.)	3. François décrit les chats comme ennuyeux parce qu'ils dorment toute la journée et griffent les meubles quand ils se réveillent. (François describes cats as boring because they sleep all day and scratch the furniture when they wake up.)	4. Le vendeur suggère qu'ils adoptent un perroquet pour résoudre leur problème. (The salesman suggests they adopt a parrot to solve their disagreement.)
B	1. Faux	2. Vrai	3. Faux	4. Faux
C	1. François veut adopter un gros chien pour garder la maison.	2. Céline préfère adopter un chat parce qu'ils sont petits, propres et mignons.		

STORY #4: Une journée à la plage

A	1. La plage est très bondée, les gens jouent de la musique forte, et il y a beaucoup d'enfants et de bébés qui pleurent. (The beach is very crowded, people are playing loud music, and there are many children and crying babies.)	2. Des châteaux de sable. (Sandcastles)	3. Les enfants leur jettent du sable et de l'eau. (The kids are throwing sand and water at them.)	4. Calme, avec beaucoup moins de monde. (Peaceful and much less crowded.)	5. Des coquillages (Seashells)
B	1. b) italienne	2. b) mer	3. b) bondée	4. a) déçus	5. b) la voiture

STORY #5: Dans la cuisine

A	1. Elles préparent un gâteau. (They're baking a cake.)	2. Elle met 4 cuillères. (She adds 4 spoonfuls.)	3. Elle tombe et le casse. (She falls and breaks it.)	4. Elle lave les bols. (She washes the bowls.)
B	1. Faux	2. Faux	3. Vrai	
C	1. La maman prend du sucre en poudre et dit : « D'abord, il faut mettre une cuillère. »	2. Après 30 minutes, Maman met le gâteau dans four.	3. Angèle coupe le gâteau avec un petit couteau et met une part dans chaque assiette.	

STORY #6: Le dîner de mariage

A	1. Marc	2. Aymen	3. Emma	4. Pauline and Eddy's parents. Les parents de Pauline et d'Eddy.
B	1. Marc va s'asseoir à côté de la cousine de Pauline.	2. Aymen va s'asseoir à côté de Thomas.	3. La tante d'Eddy va s'asseoir à côté de l'oncle de Pauline.	4. Amélie va s'asseoir à côté de Valentin.
C	1. La mère de Pauline parle toujours de ses chats	2. Le père d'Eddy préfère parler de cinéma et d'art.		

STORY #7: Mange tes fruits et tes légumes

A	1. The alien has 8 heads. L'alien a huit (8) têtes	2. L'arbre dans le ventre de Jimmy a besoin de pluie/d'eau			
B	1. C Le brocoli est un arbre	2. A Le raisin est un alien	3. B Le chou-fleur est un nuage		
C	1. Jimmy veut seulement manger des bonbons à chaque repas.	2. Julia propose à Jimmy une banane lorsqu'il refuse de manger les épinards.	3. Julia dit à Jimmy que le brocoli est en fait un arbre magique.	4. Jimmy dit que l'arbre a besoin de pluie pour vivre.	5. Après avoir mangé le brocoli et les raisins, Julia prend le chou-fleur et dit que ce sont des nuages.

STORY #8: L'Anniversaire

A	1. Il veut acheter une montre. (He wants to buy a watch.)	2. 15 euros	3. Il trouve un chapeau marron. (He finds a brown hat.)	4. Parce qu'elle a acheté une montre. (Because she bought a watch.)	5. Il chante et il danse. (He sings and dances.)
B	1. Samuel est un garçon gentil qui aime beaucoup sa famille et adore surtout faire des cadeaux.	2. Samuel compte son argent et trouve qu'il a quinze euros.	3. Il regarde dans les cartons et trouve un chapeau marron.	4. L'oncle Charlie a acheté une bouteille de vin pour l'anniversaire.	5. Le grand-père de Samuel dit que le chapeau est exactement le même que celui que sa grand-mère lui a acheté il y a 20 ans.

STORY #9: L'Echarpe Rouge d'Emily

A	1. Elle cherche son écharpe porte-bonheur. (She's looking for her lucky scarf.)	2. Il regarde la télé dans le salon. (He's watching TV in the living room.)	3. Le frère d'Emily (Emily's brother)		
B	1. C Thomas est dans la chambre	2. D Odile est dans la cuisine	3. A Olivier est dans le salon	4. B Le chien est dans le panier	
C	1. Emily cherche son écharpe rouge porte-bonheur.	2. La maman d'Emily prépare le petit-déjeuner dans la cuisine.	3. Le chien d'Emily dort dans son panier.		

Made in United States
Orlando, FL
15 December 2024